P9-DUK-577

Masters of French Literature

Masters of French Literature

BY

GEORGE McLEAN HARPER

PROFESSOR IN PRINCETON UNIVERSITY

Essay Index Reprint Series

Originally published by:

Charles Scribner's Sons

BOOKS FOR LIBRARIES PRESS, INC.

FREEPORT, NEW YORK

First published 1901
Reprinted 1968

Reprinted from a copy in the collections of
The New York Public Library
Astor, Lenox and Tilden Foundations

LIBRARY OF CONGRESS CATALOG CARD NUMBER:
68-22095

PRINTED IN THE UNITED STATES OF AMERICA

TO MY WIFE

Preface

It may not be amiss to give a preliminary hint to the reader as to the general purpose of the following essays. To the mind of their writer they possess a certain consistency, which he wishes his reader might bear in mind from the outset, rather than realize at the end or never perceive at all. So unified is French literature, so intimate are the myriad relations of all its parts to the whole, that it is possible to gain a fairly comprehensive view of any one of its periods of development by considering a representative man of letters who then was a dominant figure. What we learn from him and about him will open up vistas in all directions. We shall become acquainted no less with his environment than with the man himself. The essentials of French literary history, — the interesting and vital features, — from the eleventh century to the twentieth, might be comprised under a brief succession of illuminating titles: we may view the total landscape from a score of observatories. The "Chanson de Roland" is not a solitary peak, and from its hoary eminence we may gaze down upon the tumbled masses of the whole vast epical period, and locate them with reference to their chief. The noble group of the three mediæval chroniclers might be measured from one summit, — Villehardouin, Joinville, or Froissart. The mediæval lyric poetry would be seen sufficiently from the slender spire of aspiration which Villon reared above the mud of Paris and his own degradation. Mediæval humor and philosophy, and the dawn of the Renaissance, might be studied from the broad platform of Rabelais. The placid valley where Ronsard sang of love, and the vale where Du Bellay breathed the sweet air of Anjou, can still be made to echo the artistic questions, the debates about diction and metre, which interested the sixteenth century. A glance from the windows of Montaigne's library tower beside the Garonne might at least arouse our curiosity as to the philosophical tendencies of that age and the extent of the New Learning.

PREFACE

From five points of vantage — Pascal, La Fontaine and Boileau, Molière, Corneille and Racine, and La Bruyère and Madame de Sévigné — one might obtain a reasonably complete triangulation of the great seventeenth-century literature. The full horizon of the eighteenth century might be swept, and almost all notable French writers and literary tendencies of that important time be included, in three turns of the glass, — towards Saint-Simon and Montesquieu, towards Voltaire, and towards Rousseau. For the nineteenth century, owing to the increased diversity of the landscape, the survey would require more points of observation; and even with a very close scrutiny, there are some exalted hills and delectable valleys which would be sure to escape enumeration. Yet a rough map of the country might be sketched, from stations that should bear the names Hugo, Musset, George Sand and Dumas *père*, Sainte-Beuve, Balzac, Augier and Dumas *fils*, and Daudet and Zola. Sometimes two names would be united in one title because of a community of spirit, and sometimes because of the inviting contrast.

PREFACE

For the general reader, I fancy such a history of French literature would be far more illuminating than some of the detailed handbooks which bewilder the mind with thousands of names and titles, and brief, insufficient abstracts of books great and small. There would be the difference that exists between a series of views from twenty mountain tops, each one within sight of its immediate neighbors, and the record made by a pedometer. Or, to vary this rather prolonged figure of speech which has helped us thus far, such a history would possess the advantage that a person gains from residence in a few foreign towns, as compared with spending an equal amount of time in rapid travel, from one meaningless hotel to another.

This volume of essays, of course, makes no claim to give a general outlook over the two centuries which lie between Corneille and Balzac. Yet the book may perhaps be regarded as an imperfect illustration of the method outlined above. The absence of any substantive treatment of Rousseau and his followers would at once preclude pretension to systematic completeness, though the references to him, in the essay on Saint-Simon and Montesquieu, are designed to indicate the nature and importance of his influence.

Several of the essays are here reprinted, after more or less radical revision. Thanks are due in this connection to Messrs. Henry Holt & Company.

PRINCETON UNIVERSITY,
February, 1901.

CONTENTS

THE
PLACE OF FRENCH LITERATURE

THE

PLACE OF FRENCH LITERATURE

THE pre-eminence of French literature over its modern rivals has been complacently taken for granted by most Frenchmen. There is something not unnatural — indeed, there is something worthy of respect — in this view, even though their manner of putting it may irritate or amuse. French national vanity has been gratified by many eminent writers, from Voltaire to M. Brunetière, at no small sacrifice of true perspective. Yet they have made brilliant and interesting comparisons between their own national literary product and that of Italy, Spain, Germany, and England, and one would hesitate to blame them for drawing chiefly self-flattering conclusions, if only they were less narrow in their methods, and did not follow one another so closely in their reading of foreign works. For what value has an estimate of Italian literature which is based almost entirely upon a knowledge of Tasso and Ariosto, with Dante omitted? What ground of comparison is furnished by an acquaintance with English literature through Shakespeare, Pope, Addison, and Byron only? And what are the chances of progress in the views of French critics, if they pursue merely the traditional round of English or Italian reading?

A foreigner's conception of the place of French literature may be equally ill balanced; but if so, it will be from some other cause than inability to appreciate anything that is not French. There are several excellent reasons why it may be useful to make a survey of the general relations of French literature. It may be that we entertain a high opinion of its merits, and wish to review the grounds of our liking; or we may want to consider, in the presence of so many claims for various studies, whether it is worth while, as much as ever, to read French. To diminish the danger which such an attempt invites, we must guard against merely conventional estimates, and leave out of account those authors whom, in some mysterious way, we have come to hold in honor without having really felt their power, or perhaps even read them.

We are concerned with only so much of our own and of foreign literature as is vital to us now for purposes of general culture. Of Italian literature, a well-educated Frenchman might say Boccaccio, Tasso, and Ariosto were vital to him; but if he added Dante he would not be truly representative of his countrymen. We Americans and English, for our part, should perhaps say the "Divine Comedy," parts of the "Decameron," a very few of Petrarch's sonnets, and something of Manzoni and Leopardi; if we added Tasso and Ariosto it would be singular. Of French literature a much larger quantity is accessible to us and full of life, yet we must be careful not to speak of even such great men as Pascal, Racine, Bossuet, and Saint-Simon as if their works were really our daily bread. And we must avoid taking for granted that to Frenchmen all of English literature can mean what it does to us. Indeed, if we are frank, we shall admit that a large part of our literature has ceased to yield much sustenance even to us, whether through its remoteness or our own fault.

French literature possesses a signal advantage in the fact that a very large proportion of it is really vital to Frenchmen, and that most of what they enjoy we foreigners may also relish. It is easier in the case of

French than in the case of English to say what is literature. The national genius has led to the maintenance of a rigid censorship by the highest courts of public opinion, — the Academy, the centralized system of education, and especially the most cultivated circles of Parisian readers. A few eminent critics and a succession of women distinguished for wit and taste have been the acknowledged jurists in these matters. The conventions thus established decide between excellent and inferior work, between the permanent and the ephemeral. The debates are long and minute; but when once the boundaries are sharply fixed, no educated person in France is exempt from reading the approved authors. A time limit is also set, not so much by convention as by convenience; it is generally agreed that one is not obliged to be acquainted with much that was written before the seventeenth century, on the ground that the language of the sixteenth century was not yet really modern French.

One result of these exclusions has been to render possible and necessary for Frenchmen a comprehensiveness of reading which is relatively infrequent with us, and in this way to supply, as it were, a national subject of thought, a national topic of conversation, a national fund of common interests. You can seldom be sure that more than a small minority of an English or American audience will appreciate a literary allusion; for though every one in the room may be well read, there is no telling just what he has read. In France you may quote from the canonized list of approved authors with full assurance of being understood by all educated persons.

Another result is that some tincture of literary taste and accomplishment has penetrated lower in the social mass than with us. Most French people, above the merely illiterate, do actually know something of their literature for the last three hundred years. They go to hear the plays of Racine, Corneille, Molière, Regnard, and Beaumarchais, as well as of Dumas *fils* and Augier. They are really acquainted at first-hand, however slightly, with Pascal, La Rochefoucauld, Bossuet, La Bruyère, Madame de Sévigné, La Fontaine, Boileau, and Saint-Simon, with Montesquieu, Lesage, Voltaire, and Rousseau, as well as with the poets of 1830 and the recent novelists.

For the last three hundred years French literature has maintained a sort of corporate existence. We find in it less diversity of type than in ours; and it has been possible for one great critic to prove it to be the homogeneous product of a singularly unified people, and for another to trace the evolution of its forms. There may indeed be in the dogmatism of Taine and M. Brunetière a ruthless severity which has blinded them to whatever did not accord with their theories; but it is easy to see how the solidarity of French literature must tempt a speculative mind.

For French literature is like a family dwelling in one great mansion. We advance to knock at the front door, and a troop of lively children flock about us on the steps. They are the gay farces and sparkling comedies and the sprightly stories which have enlivened the world from Molière's time to the days of the elder Dumas, Scribe, and Labiche. At the portal, if we are wise, we shall place ourselves under the guidance of Sainte-Beuve; for no one else is so well acquainted with the family history, ancient and modern, public and private, with genealogies and titles, with deeds of prowess, and with whispered scandals. He knows to a nicety the intricate relationships of every branch, and all degrees of cousinship. In his genial society we wander on, through quiet firelit rooms where easy-slippered old gentlemen are composing memoirs, — Joinville in his honorable eld, Sully unused but active in retirement, Saint-Simon indignant, resentful, his head smoking with fervor; through the cold cells of austere Pascal and gentle François de Sales; through apartments bright with a hundred tapers, where the ladies of the Hôtel de Rambouillet, or Madame de La Fayette, or Madame Sophie Gay, or our guide's friend, Madame Récamier, receive great wits and poets. He conducts us finally to the throne room, or hall of honor, where, on gilded chairs, and with laurel-crowned brows, the family dignitaries sit in high confabulation: the king of comedy, sad-smiling Molière; the kings of tragedy, Corneille and Racine; the prince of preachers, Bossuet, with warning hand; Montaigne, asking hard questions; Rabelais, himself a riddle; La Fontaine, who chafes at so much pomp; Voltaire, whose vanity helps him endure it; Hugo, lord of many realms; noble Musset; bulky Balzac. In every countenance some lineament proclaims the family blood. Fathers here are proud to own renowned sons, and sons to claim lineage from great sires. The marks of race are not to be mistaken. Of adopted children there are a few, and in them the family traits are wanting. Rousseau, for one, is plainly not of this blood, though he does honor to the house.

When we make the acquaintance of one member, we soon learn to know many. Introductions fly from lip to lip, and before long we are at home and hospitably entertained. There is much banter and anecdote and gossip. It is a world in itself, for many inmates have never stirred abroad, and these four walls hold everything they love. Others have travelled, but with reluctance, and have always been glad to return. There is a family hierarchy and an etiquette and order of precedence very definitely settled. Several members of the household, besides Sainte-Beuve, are enthusiastic antiquarians, and their researches are continually adding vitality to the family bond.

If no other literature presents to the world so solid a front, the reason probably is that French men and women of letters, with singularly few exceptions, have really lived in personal contact. Paris, at one time or another in their careers, has contained them all. Nor have social barriers been able, as a rule, to separate those whom common talents have joined together. And the traditions of each generation have passed, through groups of intimate acquaintances, to the next. In marked contrast to these circumstances, the hearthstone of English letters has been now London, now Florence, now the northern Athens, now beside Grasmere, now Boston, and at times the flame has burned warm, but of various hues, on all at once. There is pathos indeed in Wordsworth's lament at the grave of Burns, —

> "Huge Criffel's hoary top ascends
> By Skiddaw seen, —
> Neighbors we were, and loving friends
> We might have been."

As the Brontës are of Yorkshire, so Jane Austen is of Hampshire. What an abyss in education and social feeling yawns between Charles Dickens and Walter Pater! What uncongenial couples would be Keats and Carlyle, Swinburne and Newman! How vain to attempt a search for typical English features in Shelley, Browning, or Landor, whose chief racial trait seems to be the strong determination to have none. There is scarcely a French writer that cannot be classified. But who shall put a label on Izaak Walton, Sir Thomas Browne, Jeremy Taylor, or George

Herbert, on Samuel Johnson, Gilbert White, Arthur Young, or William Blake, on Thomas Hood or Coleridge, on William Godwin or Harriet Martineau, on William Morris or the Rossettis, on George Borrow or Sir Richard Burton, on Emerson, on Thoreau, on Ruskin?

This diversity of type is but a reflection of the complex political, social, and religious life of the English-speaking world. We are Englishmen, Americans, Irish, Scotch, Welsh, Canadians, Australians; we are democrats, socialists, frontiersmen, feudal lords; we are divided into a hundred stubborn sects. Local pride is often stronger in us than national patriotism.

As both cause and effect of the unity of French literature must be noted the peculiar zeal of the French people in literary controversy. They never weary of reading and writing about those matters which, as one of their critics declares, "are always in order." That Sainte-Beuve, for instance, has discoursed charmingly on some seventeenth-century worthy is deemed no reason why M. Doumic should not approach the same subject from another side, even though, in the interval, Scherer has revealed its moral aspect, or Taine has made it illustrate his evolutionary theory. It is very properly assumed by the French that each generation, each literary school indeed, may refashion the past, because no single era can lay claim to complete knowledge or a perfect standard of judgment. And to systematize its knowledge is a necessity of the Gallic mind.

So then the French may be right in saying, as they often do, that their great authors truly represent the national life, and that in their literature has been drawn a faithful portrait of the ideal Frenchman and the ideal Frenchwoman. It is evident that no such statement can be for a moment maintained in regard to English literature. And, indeed, to maintain it at all rigidly in regard to French literature leads to strange and amusing inconsistencies. Yet not a few eminent critics, among them Taine and the estimable Nisard, have made this contention the very backbone of their teaching, — with what curious results, sometimes, the latter's "History of French Literature" may serve as an illustration. Still, it is undeniable that French literature is singularly homogeneous, and that France may well be proud of the very definite and in the main favorable representation which it gives of her character and life.

There must be something exhilarating to a Frenchman in the omnipresence of French books. In all civilized countries outside of France they enjoy a popularity second only to that of books in the native languages, if, indeed, they do not take the first place itself. I remember seeking Dutch books in the shops of Delft, and finding chiefly French. I recall that in a summer resort among the Apennines I could neither buy nor borrow an Italian novel, because everybody was reading Daudet and Zola, Bourget, Loti, and Maupassant. It is said that in the eastern states of Europe French works are even more prominent than in Holland and Italy; that in Athens, Constantinople, and the cities of Russia they far exceed all others in sale and circulation. In Norway, Sweden, and Denmark, in Spain and Portugal, in Egypt, in Mexico and South America, the French novel, the French comedy, the French book of travel or speculation, occupy at least the second rank. It is only where American, English, or German influence prevails that French writing is not thus almost or altogether paramount.

Connected with this great popularity, both as cause and effect, is the prevalence of the French language. No other modern tongue is so much studied by aliens. German is perhaps studied by a larger number of Americans, owing to the presence of a German population in our country, and to the influence of the German universities upon the last two generations of our most ambitious young scholars. But in Great Britain and throughout the rest of the world French is the favorite foreign language.

And there is another respect in which the ascendency of French letters is almost as great as this mere popular vogue. Our Anglo-Saxon civilization, by its antiquity, continuity, and vitality, is well adapted to resist foreign influence; yet it is remarkable for how much of recent progress in literary workmanship we are indebted to France. Every new phenomenon in French literature, every fresh departure in method, stimulates the development of theories in criticism. Our critics cannot afford to neglect these doctrines, and do in fact adopt them, with advantage. The French masters of the short story have given invaluable lessons to the world, in brevity, simplicity, and concentration. One has but to investigate the sources of half the new plays that appear in an English dress, to discover that they are adaptations from the French. English style is constantly being modified by French example, and often with good results in the direction of order and clearness.

In spite of these titles to our favor, perhaps it will seem that as much as has been claimed for French literature might be claimed for Italian or German. The "Divine Comedy" alone easily outweighs the entire mass of French poetry. Yet Italian literature is, as a whole, less effective than French literature. Its current has not been so continuously well supplied. In prose it is comparatively very poor. For much of Italian prose is singularly unlike what one would expect the thought of Dante's countrymen to be; it is languid and obscure, not quick and vigorous. Much of it is deficient in intellectual substance. Nevertheless, the one man Dante and his incomparable poem suffice to keep Italian literature forever in the front rank.

For all the charm of German poetry,— and its charm is deep, and clings in memory like music loved in childhood,—for all the tenderness and depth, the homely warmth and kind simplicity, which make German poetry so dear to us, I am not sure but that French prose is more likely to do us good. There is in our own poetry much that may enlarge our capacity for sentiment. And this, moreover, is not what we need so much as something to sharpen our purely intellectual faculties, — something not at all abundant in our own, but almost superabundant in French literature. To make precise distinctions, to observe rules, to cultivate artistic clearness, — these are habits which we may acquire by reading French prose.

Italian and German thought, especially as expressed in poetry, have again and again been the refuge and inspiration of our great English writers; but the influence of French literature has been more constant and broader. It has reached us all. Considering both quantity and quality, both good effects and bad, it is surely no exaggeration to say that French ideas and French fashions of writing have invaded the English mind and English letters more than have the thoughts and style of any other nation except the Hebrew.

The pre-eminence of French literature in the non-English world has been so unquestioned that much of English literature, although at least as excellent, has been obscured and relegated to a second place. It would not be impossible, perhaps, to maintain the proposition that ours, in depth and seriousness, in scope and variety, is the greater literature of the two, and indeed superior to any other since the Greek. Yet whereas, for most educated people on the Continent, Milton is only a name, and Wordsworth, Shelley, Keats, Burke, Thackeray, Hawthorne, and Ruskin are but shadows, Montaigne, Molière, Montesquieu, Voltaire, Rousseau, Hugo, Balzac, have wrought a mighty work in political and social life, and their thought is being woven, night and day, into the complex tissue of European civilization. There must be some peculiar quality in French literature which has made it thus universally pervasive. If it has been received by all other European peoples as their favorite foreign body of thought, the cause must be its adaptability to the minds of all men. It must be that it abounds in general and easily comprehended excellences. It must be closely connected with the unvarying realities of life. It must be remarkably normal to the average human intelligence.

In short, if French literature is universally pervasive, it is because it is universally applicable.

The character of a thing depends upon its origin, its environment, and the special mode or instrument employed in its production. The origin of French literature is in the minds of Frenchmen, and when comparing general traits we may speak collectively of the French mind. The environment in which this literature has been created, and by which it has been modified, is the life of the French people. The special instrument employed is the French language. So, to apprehend the causes of the peculiar adaptability of French literature to the world's need, we may not unreasonably seek them in these three factors, — French character, French history, and the French tongue.

And considering first the character of the average Frenchman to-day and in the past, and the nature of French society, we observe the same centrality which we have remarked in the literature. The French think straight. Their minds work along the lines of normal universal logic, in company with one another, above ground, in the full sunlight; not by labored processes, through subterranean caverns, as German minds do; not erratically, like a river, now hiding in the sands, then sparkling forth again, as do Russian minds; not paddling along in personal seclusion, like tortoises, each with his own house on his back, as do the minds of Englishmen. French thought is simple and direct, and so are French manners. This is why the etiquette of French society has become the accepted form of intercourse in most other civilized countries. It is a mistake to think of the French as excessive or artificial in their expression of politeness. It is rather in German, Scandinavian, and Spanish social circles that unreasonable formalities persist. And two French traits — traits, moreover, which have a close connection with literary production — are the desire to please and the artistic instinct. The Frenchman is fond of producing satisfaction, — partly from genuine kindliness, and partly because it reflects credit upon himself. His artistic instinct comes to the aid of his love of pleasing, so that if he wishes to give flowers to a lady, he will not thrust them at her, in an awkward handful, but lay them gracefully at her feet, in a well-ordered bouquet. If he has occasion to sing a song, or ride a horse, or write a letter, he will be at pains to avoid a shabby performance. He would be humiliated if he misspelled a word or wrote it illegibly.

Thus the French seek for their thought an interesting form, lucid, readily diffusible, and therefore practical. They are led naturally to a dramatic rather than a philosophical expression of their thought, because the dramatic form is more immediately telling. Their thought is expressed also in general rather than technical terms, and is therefore more widely understood. It aims at simplicity rather than completeness, and thus avoids anything like pedantry. French thought may often be vague and peculiar enough before it has reached artistic expression, but when moulded into form it stands out free from eccentricity. Whatever is fantastic is not French. The French have also a horror of obtrusive individuality, and one of their strongest terms of reprobation is to say of a man, " C'est un original." It is in a measure true of them, and truer of them, perhaps, than of any other people, that

> " The individual withers, and the world is more and more."

Of the second factor, the environment, determined chiefly by political change, by history, it is enough to say that in the three great phases of institutional development since the fall of the Roman Empire — feudalism, absolutism, democracy — France has been the initiatory and typical example. The feudal system was first and most fully developed in France, and introduced thence into England at the Conquest. It was Louis XI. who first broke the power of the barons, in which feudalism consisted, and Louis XIV. who perfected his work and became the most absolute personal sovereign that western Europe has known. It was the French philosophers of the eighteenth century who undermined the royal power in France, and through Thomas Jefferson, Thomas Paine, and Benjamin Franklin effected the theoretical preparations for the American Revolution, which otherwise might indeed have been an armed protest against taxation, but would hardly have resulted in a refusal, on principle, of allegiance to King George. The slower process of reform by act of Parliament has, to be sure, given the England of to-day a freer government than republican France possesses or has ever possessed; but it must not be forgotten that the American Revolution and the French Revolution forced the tardy hand of English legislation, and that many solid British liberties, acquired in peace and quietness, are indirectly due to the "red fool-fury of the Seine."

Until recently, French affairs have ever been foremost in European politics, and to write of French kings or French generals or French diplomacy has been to address the world on subjects in which it was interested. Thus we may attribute to French history the same quality of centrality which we found to belong to French character, and once more infer that this may well be a cause of the universal applicability and acceptability of French literature.

In one great historical movement, however, France has not occupied as prominent a place as Germany and England; namely, in the religious and moral Reformation which became widespread in the sixteenth century, and is still operative in all Teutonic countries. Every attempt to establish generally the reformed principles in France has been crushed by the arm of despotism, or thwarted by the folly and shallowness of Protestant nobles, or nullified by the lukewarmness and moral feebleness of the middle classes. To the failure of France to grasp her opportunities in this respect, I believe we must attribute a decadence, moral and physical, which is becoming precipitate, and which bids fair to reduce her to a secondary rank among nations.

A third cause of the universality and popularity of French literature is the fitness of the French language. To it, also, as to French character and French history, we may apply the words "central" and "normal." Its grammar is simple, — though not so simple as that of Italian or Spanish. Its vocabulary, in which the Latin originals are often clearly discernible, is easy to acquire and retain. Its orthography, while not phonetic, is based on rigid principles, the same combination of letters being, with rare exceptions, always pronounced alike. The firmness of its mechanism makes French a satisfactory language to foreigners. There is usually some one accepted way of expressing a given idea, and the idioms are so striking that, once thoroughly learned, they are never forgotten.

It is only the degenerate writers of our own time, the so-called naturalists, who have gathered slang and thieves' jargon from the gutters of Paris and attempted to force them into good company, and the half-crazed decadent poets, who, in their ignoble scramble for notoriety, have invented meaningless phrases, — it is only through the deliberate efforts of these men that the French language has suffered any radical change in the last three hundred years. For the Romanticists of 1830, while, it is true, they enriched the vocabulary of poetry, did so mainly by reviving certain ancient and half-forgotten but thoroughly French expressions, and admitting these and many terms of the prose or colloquial language into the "consecrated" list of words allowable in verse. As a rule they took no improper liberties with syntax, and did not cultivate either obscurity or slang. You can read Molière more easily than you can read Paul Verlaine; and the vocabulary of Zola is vastly larger and more unfamiliar than that of Saint-Simon and Voltaire. In short, until the last forty years there has been no very serious alteration in either the grammar or the vocabulary since the close of the sixteenth century; so that it has been eminently worth while to know French, because a command of the language enabled one to read indiscriminately in the literature of the last three hundred years. It is interesting to observe that Old French, also, or the language as written from the middle of the eleventh to the beginning of the sixteenth century, preserved a character of remarkable uniformity for nearly five hundred years.

The case of English has been quite different. A foreigner who can read Byron, Addison, and Washington Irving may not know the language well enough to understand Dickens or Carlyle, Shelley or Swinburne. Nor is the ability to read the simple love songs of Heine a guarantee that one can even make sense out of Schiller's noble ballads or Goethe's intricate and learned prose.

It is not likely, however, that the modern innovators will be able to corrupt permanently the French language, so clear, facile, and solidly constructed. It will probably continue to resist the encroachments of personal and local idiosyncrasy. It is still amply protected by the Academy, and by the traditions of the University and the National Theatre.

We read in the writings of Wace, a Norman-English poet, that the French bard Taillefer went into the battle of Hastings singing of Charlemagne and Roland. What he sang was probably from the "Chanson de Roland," composed most likely, in some form or other, before the middle of the eleventh century.

And the "Chanson de Roland" was but one of many epic poems that grew up in France at the same time. Thus French literature is much more ancient than Italian literature and English literature. For it is fair to admit that English literature does not begin before the age of Chaucer. The Anglo-Saxon language, although modern English is bone of its bone, differs from modern English so widely that for practical purposes it is another tongue. We cannot read "Beowulf" or the "Saxon Chronicle" or Alfred without long and serious preparation, any more than we could read Dutch or Norwegian; but this earliest French, the French of the "Chanson de Roland," wears the physiognomy of modern French. A French schoolboy, with intelligence and patience, can make out its meaning. We do not have to give it another name, as we do Anglo-Saxon. It is French.

What is still more remarkable, from the earliest times of its history, eight hundred and fifty years ago, there has been no break in the seamless unity of French literature. Its characteristics have been the same from age to age. It has been a living organism, marked by the same excellences, the same defects, at all stages of its development.

Take it at any point you will, and you must find it interesting, full of life, vividly concerning itself with contemporary history. M. Brunetière, in his fine essay entitled "Le Caractère essentiel de la Littérature française," sums up the distinguishing quality of French literature in the word "social;" meaning that it has, in the main, and more than other literatures, been produced with direct consideration of the tastes and needs of an immediate circle of readers. The appropriateness of M. Brunetière's remark becomes apparent when we consider what a large part of French literature consists of letters, memoirs, literary criticism, comedies, and dramas of private life. I would go a step farther than M. Brunetière, and say that French literature is not only social, but appeals to the taste of a high and aristocratic society. It is marked by a noble distinction and courtly grace. It has the urbane quality which comes from city life. It has that lucidity, that definiteness and positiveness, which seem also to be the results of high-pressure existence in a metropolis.

On the other hand, its deficiencies, as compared with English literature, seem to be a want of variety and freedom, a want of depth too, which three qualities, I think, — variety, freedom, and depth, — are the glory of English literature. The remarkable thing is that it has maintained its character from first to last, so that one studying the poems of Charles d'Orléans and Villon in the fifteenth century finds them, in spirit and weight, curiously like the poems of Théophile Gautier and Alfred de Musset in our own day. This majestic fulness and this sustained identity of character are mainly due to the fact that the French have been, generally speaking, a very homogeneous and united people, — one in religion, in patriotic ideals, and in social impulses.

Moreover, it is not merely in recent times that French literature has maintained either the supremacy as compared with other modern literatures, or at least a position in the first rank. It has been of such a sort that if you wish to know what the choice spirits of the world were thinking, at any given time, about the most important contemporary happenings, you will not be far astray if you read the French books of that period. The position of French literature has all along been much like the geographical situation of the country, in the centre of western Europe, or like the political standing of the nation, in the forefront of progress. To be imbued with the French spirit has almost always meant to be near the heart of the age. And furthermore, French literature has shared with Italian the distinction of being a large part of the channel through which Greek and Roman civilization and the traditions of ancient scholarship have flowed downward into the modern world.

All this immense success has not been achieved without conscious effort. It has not all been due to impersonal causes. Nowhere has literary competition been so severe as in France. Nowhere has good work been so openly and dazzlingly rewarded. And nowhere, also, has failure been so quickly remarked and unhesitatingly derided. So that, in order to receive the stamp of authoritative approval, literary work in France has had to come up to a high standard. Frenchmen have the artistic conscience more highly developed than Englishmen or Germans, and are less likely to commend a badly written book or a poor painting. It is the carefulness resulting from such sharp competition and such outspoken criticism that, more than anything else, has made French prose so clear, until now it is perhaps a more easily handled instrument of expression than English, and certainly more facile than German, and more precise than Italian.

There are certain fields in which the pre-eminence of French literature is acknowledged. It holds the palm for memoirs and letters, for criticism, and for comedy. It is doubtful whether any other periods of history are so abundantly and entertainingly represented in correspondence and diaries as the age of Louis XIV., the Regency, and the reign of Louis XV. Something comparable, indeed, has been done for the age of Queen Anne by English men of letters; but the feminine element here is not sufficiently prominent, and the scene, while not lacking in color, is too vaguely outlined. We have had one literary critic of the very first rank in Matthew Arnold, and many men of genius, like Coleridge and Lamb, who were great critics occasionally. But, in general, criticism has not been viewed seriously among us, as one of the grand, natural, necessary, and distinct divisions of literature. Even Lowell, with his eminent critical gift, was too often willing to lower the tone of an essay by admitting a pun or other irrelevancy. What we need as much perhaps as we need great critics of the first rank, and what can be more easily supplied, is a sound tradition, in which minor reviewers may grow into usefulness; a standard or standards which shall promote consistency, or at least define real issues. As compared with the chaos in America and England, criticism has, in France, reached the development of a fine art. What exalted names are Geoffroy, Villemain, Sainte-Beuve, Planche, Scherer, and Taine, to mention only the dead! What an abundance, what a superabundance, of schools and methods have we seen there even in our own day!

Yet we too have had some critics, as we have had some letter-writers and diarists. But what must be said of English comedy as compared with French comedy? It is practically non-existent, so far as present vitality is concerned, except for Shakespeare, Goldsmith, and Sheridan. Meanwhile, for every phase in the development of French society, during the last three centuries, there has been an accompanying comment in the form of comedy, which is capable of being made the most useful of all arts, from a moral and social point of view. The history of the French people for the last three hundred years may be traced in their comedies. And their comedies have helped to make history. "Le

Mariage de Figaro" was worth more to the revolutionary cause than ten barricades or ten thousand bayonets. At every point, in this long period, we find French comedy still vital. The ancients are as popular as the moderns: "Tartufe," "Le Joueur," "Le Barbier de Séville," see the footlights as often as "Le Fils de Giboyer" and "La Dame aux Camélias." Moreover, these lively creations appeal not only to the French but to us all.

Perhaps it is that the French take more seriously to light things than we do, and make serious successes out of what with us are only light attempts; whatever the cause, they excel us in comedy, criticism, and the epistolary art. But in spite of enormous effort and productiveness by the French in prose fiction, it may be said, though not, of course, without risk of contradiction, that the English novel, and also the Russian novel, present nobler and more varied and especially truer types of men and women, and a vastly wider range of action. The almost exclusive preoccupation of French novelists has been and is the study of sexual relations, preferably immoral. The rest of life does not attract them. The spacious world of masculine strife for power seems to them small in comparison. The miniature world of home, vital and common to all, they have despised, in favor of a demi-monde which one cannot help suspecting them of having rather created than observed. Woman they have abundantly, though discouragingly, portrayed. But there is scarcely a man in French fiction, let alone a gentleman. Outdoor life, physical danger and prowess, the joy of muscular effort and victory over things, the glory of self-control, the intoxication of free movement amid nature's terrible and fascinating sport, — all these are infinitely better and more copiously rendered by Gogol and Tolstoi, by Fielding, Scott, and Stevenson, than by any Frenchman; for Dumas is frankly and happily unnatural, and the sentimentality of George Sand, Hugo, and Loti tinges with false color so many a page that the sense of reality is subtly impaired in all their novels. Nor, apart from the description of sexual emotions, and apart from Balzac, has French literature a master of social synthesis to compare with Jane Austen, Thackeray, or Trollope, or with Turgenieff. And for novels of psychological analysis, with the same exceptions, there is no French diviner of the heart like Hawthorne and

George Eliot; for Stendhal is dreary, and Bourget chooses for the most part to limit his fine powers to studying the wearisome question of illicit love. Balzac alone of French novelists is great in a world-wide sense, but the traveller through the city of his creation needs a cicerone to save time.

In no field have the French so plumed themselves and made such determined effort, as in tragedy. Yet to most foreigners, even to many who are entirely sympathetic in their general attitude towards French literature, and to a considerable number of Frenchmen, their tragedy seems a far less imposing achievement than the tragedy of England, or even of Germany. Perhaps the cause of the comparative failure here lies in peculiar qualities of the language,—its want of natural rhythm, and the absence of a natural division in its diction between homely words and merely rhetorical words. Perhaps it lies deeper,—in the racial aversion to individuality. Parts of Corneille and Hugo, and all of Molière's real tragedy, "Le Misanthrope," and Alfred de Musset's little *proverbe*, "On ne Badine pas avec l'Amour," are tragic in a universal, and not merely French sense; but the regular French tragedy, the tragedy of Racine especially, however perfect of its kind, is not world-wide in its appeal. Its beauties, recondite, and more closely connected with form than with sense, can rarely be appreciated by foreigners. It is a *genre* apart. Possibly it would be unfair to say that the *genre* as such is less noble than the romantic tragedy of England and Germany.

In lyric and epic poetry it is the same causes which account for the same or even a more marked inferiority. Life purely social may produce charming *vers de société*, exquisite *émaux et camées*, — may produce even, as its fine flower, the fables of La Fontaine; but only a land of intellectual and moral Protestantism, a land of warm personal religious conviction, a land where the individual feels himself standing alone, with the abyss of hell below him and the eternal heaven within his reach above, can give us the "Divine Comedy" or the "Ode to Duty." The French poems which can be compared, not with the poems of Dante, Goethe, and Wordsworth, or with those of Milton, Shelley, and Keats, but with the love-songs of Germany, the plaintive monologues of Leopardi, the hundreds of minor English lyrics whose sweet undertone has been unbroken for six hundred years, are few indeed: three or four superb things by Villon in the fifteenth century, six or eight by Ronsard and Du Bellay in the sixteenth, nothing in the seventeenth, nothing in the eighteenth till we come to André de Chénier, who was half a Greek! To deny that France is great in poetry is to deny that she is great in the better half of literature. Yet in poetry English holds the primacy, with Italy a noble second, and Germany third. In the nineteenth century, however, there has been a very extensive production of what the non-French world recognizes as poetry in a universal sense, due primarily to the lyrical genius of Hugo and to the romantic school.

It is unnecessary to dwell further on the importance of French literature. Even though it were not so valuable, it would be attractive still, and men would read it for its immense resources of entertainment. And having once made ourselves acquainted with it, we shall realize its nobler qualities, shall acknowledge how sane and curative it is, what an antidote to morbidness of many sorts, what an enemy of melancholy and fanaticism, how it will preserve the mind from vain excesses and confusion and dull sloth.

THE

GOLDEN AGE OF FRENCH DRAMA

THE

GOLDEN AGE OF FRENCH DRAMA

WHEN Voltaire was asked to write a commentary on Racine he responded: "There is no commentary needed in this case. All that I could do would be to put at the bottom of each page the words Beautiful, harmonious, admirable, pathetic, sublime." This was said, no doubt, in a burst of generous appreciation, and possibly Voltaire felt for the moment that it was futile to comment on what has no defects. "A perfect being can have no parts" was a maxim of the schools. It is just as well to remember, however, that no man understood better than Voltaire the usefulness of criticism, and that he did, at one time and another, have a great deal to say about Racine. Still, it stands to reason that in the case of the drama no amount of description and praise can equal the advantages of a comfortable orchestra stall. This is true even of the extremely literary tragedies of Corneille and Racine. It is in the theatre and under the spell of the artificial sense of reality prevailing there that they stir us most deeply, though even when read aloud or declaimed amid the merest suggestion of dramatic environment, they still move our hearts, and their characters seem like creatures of a nobler world than ours, breathing diviner speech.

I confess, that to me Racine, at least, had never come home with power and charm, that although I appreciated somewhat of the tender and exquisite beauty of his language, I had never yielded to his dramatic force, until I heard his tragedy "Mithridate," at the Comédie Française. I had been listening, a few nights before, to Victor Hugo's "Hernani" at the same theatre. In "Hernani" everything which stage artifice affords had been employed to captivate the sense. The scene had swarmed with glittering figures in constant and striking action, fifty or sixty actors, great and small. We had had, in this modern romantic tragedy, a lady's apartments in a palace in Saragossa, a balcony scene, an old castle in the mountains of Aragon, with its grand hall covered with family portraits, then the tomb of Charlemagne in the crypt at Aix la Chapelle, and then a garden festival in Saragossa again. We had had moonlight rudely driven from high chamber casements by the glare of torches. Darkness and daylight had succeeded each other with more than natural effectiveness. There had been the flash and sparkle of swords crossed in combat. There had been two lyric deaths. The whole storehouse of dramatic accessories had been laid under contribution for characters, costumes, action, scenery, light and shade, and I had felt when all was over that at least no device had been left untried, in the presentation of this nineteenth century work, for producing a complete dramatic illusion.

And then, as I have said, some good genius led me, a few nights later, to hear Racine's "Mithridate," at the same theatre. I went in no very eager mood, and partly from a sense of duty, prepared to pass a tedious evening. There are only seven characters in "Mithridate," and the supernumeraries are not beautiful court ladies or charming pages, but only a squad of palace guards, who looked, on this occasion, like painted wooden soldiers. The scenery and stage setting represented a single plain room in an Oriental palace, with a view of the sea, and were the same throughout the play. A table, two chairs, and a stool were the only furniture, and their positions never varied. There was no action, beyond the necessary entrances, exits, and gestures, except the death of Mithridate, the Asiatic king, which, moreover, was performed with decorum and without undignified struggles. You could hardly imagine anything simpler, anything less dependent upon artificial aid, than this tragedy. The dialogue and the declamation stood almost alone. And yet I was completely captivated, as I had not been by "Hernani." For the dialogue was in language so pure, so lofty, so noble, so refined, and especially so unfalteringly true to itself at all points, that I seemed to be hearing some exquisite music of the older school, something like Gluck's "Eurydice;" and these soft yet dignified measures were spoken in such silvery tones as one hears only on the French stage, or from the lips of Ellen Terry in English. The crowded house was hushed as it had not been for "Hernani." It was the words which held us breathless — the words and the sentiments, not the slender thread of incident, and certainly there was no unnecessary decoration to claim our attention. I for one, and I think many hundreds like me, did not awake from the spell until we found ourselves in the noisy square outside.

Plainly no such effect can be produced by talking or writing about Racine and Corneille and analyzing their works. If you would feel the beauty of their plays, you must hear them recited on the stage or at least read aloud. In the case of Molière also, though private reading of him is delightful, yet, of course, the French comedians are his best interpreters.

But what criticism may at least attempt, is to show how it came to pass in the fulness of time that these three men of the same generation rewarded the hopes of centuries, gathered to themselves the experience of many writers who had failed, caught the ear and won the approval of their own age, and established themselves among the greatest of their race. A remarkably favorable combination of political and social causes came into sudden activity near the middle of the seventeenth century in France, and operating with extraordinary success for a few years, left a very characteristic literary product. Of this the drama is a small part quantitatively, but perhaps of more enduring interest than all the rest.

Louis XIV. came to the throne in 1643, at the age of five, and began to rule in person in 1661. Roughly speaking, the two centuries between the accession of Louis XI. in 1461, and the virtual beginning of Louis XIVth's reign, in 1661, may be considered to include the disintegration of the feudal system and the rise of absolutism. The process was more complete in France than in England. There has never really been a period of absolutism in England. During these two hundred years, from the accession of Louis XI. in 1461, to the assumption of real power by Louis XIV. in 1661, a standard of life, in manners, in art, and in government, was being formed. This standard of life was brought to perfection and exercised full authority in the strong, successful years of Louis XIV., the twenty-two years from 1661 to 1683.

When he began to rule personally, after the death of Mazarin, his prime minister and the virtual regent during his minority, the friends of peace and order hoped that he might prove a strong king, even though he should be a tyrant. The convulsions of religious war had been stilled by the popularity and manly strength of his grandfather, Henry IV., and France had been held quiet for a few years by the great minister Sully and the great minister Richelieu. But she had relapsed into violent disorder again, in the civil war called the Fronde, and the accompanying anarchy, between Richelieu's death, in 1642, and the memorable year 1661, when Louis XIV. took control of the government. So there was little opposition, and in most quarters great satisfaction, when the young king seized the occasion prepared for him by the failures of other men and the long results of time, and settled himself securely in his throne as an absolute monarch. Firmness and activity marked the beginning of his powerful rule. He was a tyrant, but he established order. The stability of the throne became an unquestionable fact. The unity of the nation was assured by the king's supremacy. There was an immediate cessation of religious strife, and Church and Throne became each the other's guarantee. An administrative system was developed, minute in detail, but simple in its original source of authority, the king's will. Paris became more than ever the heart of France.

A highly organized court life centred in the masterful monarch. Thus was constituted the governmental and social fabric which was the sensible manifestation of the idea of absolutism, an idea that had been taking shape ever since the beginning of the Renaissance.

To get an adequate conception of what this absolutism meant, it is not enough to remember that ministers, generals, and the civil and military officials under them, derived their authority directly from the sovereign. We must observe that all activity was supposed to await his bidding and look to him for reward. His honor was concerned in everything. Success of all kinds, no matter by whom achieved, was laid as a trophy at his feet. There was supposed to be real solidarity between the king and all the interests of his realm. In nothing is this better illustrated than in his relation to literature. Almost all the writers of his time were sooner or later admitted to court, and received personally his encouragement or blame. He did not hesitate to propose new subjects for their pens, and his suggestions were, of course, commands. He boldly criticised their plays and poems; and the chief sign that they really respected his opinion is the almost total absence of resentment, even in their private letters, so far as these have come down to us. The king won their attention and adhesion no less by the liberal pensions he granted to authors, than by his frank and, in the main, just and liberal criticism. Such breadth of view was natural to him, and was increased by the moral strengthening which came to him from the long exercise of his great office.

There is probably no other point in modern history which can be so well called the culminating point of a long period as the point in French history when Louis XIV. began to rule in person. There is probably no other time when a definite national ideal has taken shape so fully and expressed itself so broadly and along so many lines. The system of life under Louis XIV. was perfect of its kind. Granting the divine right of an absolute monarch at all, it must be admitted that perfection was attained during this reign in most of the forms of national greatness. In manners as in administration, in language as in dress and etiquette, in thought, finally, and in literature, the tone is the same, and it is the grand tone.

The unfailing presence and abundance of the grand tone is what distinguishes the literature of that age. It is its grand tone which gives this literature a position of authority, and makes us say of it that it is classical. It was royal in purpose and use. It was produced, much of it, directly for the king's approval, and in accordance with what was supposed to be his taste. And it has the good qualities of royalty. It is marked by decorum, reserve, dignity. It has the aristocratic habit of reverent retrospection upon what is best in the past, with an easy disregard very often for what is pressing and clamorous in the present. It has polish, fineness, wit, just enough erudition, not too much vigor. Louis himself was not more elevated — or more insufficient. Within quite narrow limits, it comprises many beautiful and admirable achievements. Among the noblest and most enduring works in French philosophy are the "Pensées" and the "Lettres provinciales" of Pascal, the profoundest thinker of that age. The most inspiring eloquence that the French language boasts is in the addresses of Bossuet, the chief court preacher under Louis XIV. Among the first great and epoch-making works in French literary criticism is the "Art poétique" of Boileau, who was distinctly a poet of the court, and held officially the position of court historian.

In these three departments of literature, in philosophy, oratory, and criticism, that is the classical age, and the works produced then are the classical or standard works. These works may be assailed. Men may deny their conclusions, and the spirit of our time may be wholly hostile to their spirit; but the form, the tone, the style, are beyond criticism, and the greatness of their influence is unquestioned. They must always be reckoned with. And they are all stamped with the same character. They are what might have been expected from an era whose distinguishing quality was love of grandeur. They are strictly in the spirit of court society under an absolute monarch.

But if this is the case with philosophy, oratory, and criticism, if they were thus conditioned by the peculiar social system of the time, may we not expect it to determine to a still larger extent the character of the drama? For of all forms of literature, the drama is most subject to contemporary influence. Plays intended for the stage have always been written in direct response to a public demand, expressed or unexpressed. Goethe's "Faust" is perhaps the only drama of first-rate excellence which was not written with a primary view to being acted, rather than read. The two men in modern times who have succeeded in creating the best dramas for the closet as well as for the stage, Shakespeare and Molière, probably wrote for some years with scarcely a thought of publishing their works. They were actors and managers of stock companies, and wrote to supply plays for immediate acting. And by serving well their age they served all time. Molière was forced into printing, much against his will, to protect himself against "pirated" editions, as he tells us in the preface to "Les Précieuses ridicules."

So we are not surprised to find that the drama of the seventeenth century in France is as full of the spirit of the age, as vibrant with the note of grandeur, as either its philosophy, or its oratory, or its criticism. It was produced for that age, not for ours. And it breathes the spirit of that age. The dramatist is by nature and calling a man of the world. Fashionable society, the people who enjoy the finest opportunities, may not always receive him, but he has within him, if he be a born dramatist, the faculty of comprehending society. Shakespeare, we may surmise, would have been an ornament to the court of England. No high-bred gentleman there would have excelled him in sweet and dignified bearing, in quick, fine perception, in appropriate conduct. Corneille and Racine, and the strolling player Molière, when they were put to the test of association with the court, proved themselves, as occasion demanded, the social peers of the Bourbons and the Montmorencis, and the equals, in dignity and grace, of any duke in the realm. This was not so much because they were poets, for there have been, here and there in the world, by some strange and unhappy chance, underbred poets. It was rather because they had the dramatist's eye for human conduct. Social distinctions, delicate shades of etiquette, and fine points of speech and action, which to many men are almost imperceptible, are enlarged as by a microscope, under the dramatist's faculty of observation. Whether or not, then, he be admitted to fellowship with the most characteristic and interesting people of his time, he is generally fit to be admitted; and in any case, even though it be but through half-open doors, he observes and judges. Corneille and Racine were allowed to enter freely into what was esteemed the best society. Shakespeare and Molière only caught glimpses of it; but their quick eyes and comprehensive minds penetrated and understood its complexities at once. The drama, furthermore, is of necessity a representation of contemporary life. Shakespeare may put Cæsar and Brutus and the Roman Senate on the stage, but they speak the thoughts and use the language of the English statesmen of his day. Bottom and Quince and Snug and Starveling, in the "Midsummer Night's Dream," are as cockney a set of mechanics as ever ate English beef and drank English ale.

Realizing this intimate connection between the drama and contemporary life, Louis XIV. and his court more consciously fostered the player's art than any other. And of all the art-products of that age, its drama is the most typical, the most representative. The perfection of absolutism is nowhere better pictured for us than in the plays of Corneille, Racine, and Molière. The best side of that life is, of course, given more prominence than the worst, — a fortunate circumstance, for we thus possess what was best in an age distinguished for dignity and measure, for elevation and grandeur of tone; we thus possess that quintessence of noble qualities which constitutes the classical French drama. And the classical drama is the noblest and most characteristic product of the French mind.

The achievement is excellent, though slender. No one but a Frenchman will claim for the classical drama that it is a broad, full representation of human life, especially on the side of tragedy. Few critics, except French critics, will admit that it is poetry of the highest order. But its perfection within certain limits is what we must all feel. In the tragedies of Corneille and Racine it is not universal human nature we are called to contemplate, but a certain restricted caste of men and women, greatly idealized, their virtues magnified, their common or ugly features unrevealed. Whether the story be of Nero's court, as in Racine's "Britannicus," or of republican Rome, as in Corneille's "Horace," or of the early Christian martyrs, as in his "Polyeucte," or out of the Old Testament, as in Racine's "Athalie" and

"Esther," the character and spirit, the philosophy of life, the etiquette and language, are inevitably those of the seventeenth century in France,, though often so much idealized as to be scarcely recognizable. So that in these plays, which are nearly all historical, or semi-historical, we have not really a picture-gallery representing life in Greece and Rome and Asia Minor, any more than the religious paintings of the old Italian and Dutch masters give us real Oriental faces, dress, and customs. Raphael's madonnas are Italian peasant women. Rembrandt's "Supper at Emäus" is a Dutch interior. As the old masters give us in their religious paintings the life of their own times, faithfully reproduced, so the only historical element that is worth much in the seventeenth century French tragedy, in spite of Corneille's and Racine's strenuous efforts to describe antiquity, is the contemporary life displayed.

Making allowance for the fact that it is court life chiefly, the life of princes and great lords and ladies, of bishops, statesmen, and generals, and making allowance also for the fact that even this court life is idealized, it is still true that the portrait-gallery of French society under Louis XIV. is to be found in the pages of the dramatists. It is the only notable artistic reproduction of that society, except the miniatures of La Fontaine and La Bruyère. Letters and memoirs, especially the memoirs of Saint-Simon, the most important of all French memoirs, do give us a broad, but not an artistic, view.

Furthermore, these plays possess, independently of their historical value, enough intrinsic merit to make them worth reading or hearing, now and at any time. This is, after all, the essential thing in a work of art, — this is the only essential thing, — that it should yield a noble pleasure. About the nature and causes of this pleasure, it is in vain, or almost in vain, that men philosophize. We feel the pleasure, if we have the sense for art. And whatever art-work makes us feel it, that we know is excellent —

> "Beauty is truth, truth beauty, — that is all
> Ye know on earth, and all ye need to know."

The classical French drama yields this noble pleasure in unceasing abundance. Therein lies its exceeding greatness.

But we shall scarcely realize how great it

is until we take a glance (and a glance will suffice) at the long, hard effort that had been made through previous ages to produce good drama in France, and the miserable failures of other men before Corneille, and consider how little there was in the traditions of the French stage to guide him.

In the Middle Ages, a species of tragedy was produced on religious holidays, before the doors, or even in the aisles, of churches. The actors were originally priests, and the subjects were stories from the Bible and from the lives of saints. The former were called mysteries, the latter miracles. Besides the churchmen, who at first held a monopoly of acting, associations of laymen, of which the latest and most celebrated was called the "Confrérie de la Passion," received permission to produce religious plays. These mysteries and miracles were the beginnings of French tragedy. Two other voluntary associations, one of gay young gentlemen, called the "Enfants sans Souci," the other of law students, called the "Clercs de la Basoche," were permitted to produce farces, which were mainly satirical, and which often for that reason occasioned trouble. In these farces we see the rudiments of French comedy. The "Clercs de la Basoche" had also the privilege of playing a fourth variety of dialogue, called "Morality," which, like the modern melodrama, was neither strictly tragic nor wholly comic. In all these performances the sole object was to impress an audience. There is little evidence of an effort to produce what would be worth reading. The art is coarse and elementary. It is not surprising, therefore, that they fell into disrepute as soon as men with some knowledge of Aristophanes and Seneca began to write.

And this is what occurred about the middle of the sixteenth century. A group of seven persons, calling themselves the Pléiade, undertook to introduce in France plays of greater intricacy and higher finish than the old-fashioned kind. Their efforts in dramatic criticism and dramatic composition were only a part of their general plan of reforming the French language and calling attention to the standards of literary excellence established by Greek and Roman authors. Ronsard in 1549 translated the "Plutus" of Aristophanes, and Jodelle, another member of the Pléiade, brought out a play, "Cléopâtre," closely copied from Greek models. The first person outside of the Pléiade to follow their example was Garnier, who imitated Seneca, and wrote nine very stupid didactic tragedies. None of these pedantic works touched the public. To reach a popular audience, and at the same time to improve on the old Mysteries, Farces, and Moralities, was the achievement of the last great predecessor of Corneille, Alexandre Hardy, who was born in 1560 and died in 1631. It is significant, that by the time of Hardy's death, Corneille was twenty-five years old, and had already, two years before, brought out a good comedy, "Mélite." Hardy wrote, it is said, more than six hundred plays. Some accounts put the number as high as twelve hundred. They were mostly close imitations from the Italian and Spanish. He wrote for a certain company of actors who were satisfied if a piece ran for a week.

Such were the wretched antecedents of the great French drama of the seventeenth century, — in the beginning rude and almost barbarous, though original; in the sixteenth century and up to Corneille, nothing but pedantic attempts to copy Seneca's second-rate imitations of the Greek, or cheap, unscrupulous adaptations of Italian and Spanish playwrights, who themselves wrote with facility and power, rather than with true art. The only play from that dim, helpless confusion and chaos of struggle that, so far as I know, is ever acted now, or even read by any except the curious, is the farce "L'Avocat Pathelin," which has been adapted for the modern stage.

The originality of Corneille can be appreciated only after some such backward turning of the leaves as we have been making, into the dullest chapters of French literature. He began to write much after the old manner, having been aroused, like his unworthy predecessors, by admiration for the cleverness of Spanish plots. It is interesting to observe how his native force of character led him, step by step, to abandon one old and stupid device after another, and to imitate better things and in a better way, until finally imitation became only an incident, and originality the general rule with him.

Pierre Corneille was born in the grand old town of Rouen, the city upon which, more than almost any other place in France, has been stamped the daring genius of the Middle Ages; for the Gothic architecture, which was the most characteristic art product of the Middle Ages, is more abundantly represented in Rouen than anywhere else. In 1606, when the poet was born, there was more of this noble architecture still standing in Rouen than we can see there to-day, and I do not think it fanciful to suppose that a susceptible boy, who was to be a poet, would be influenced for originality and sturdy power by the daily contemplation of the mighty walls of a Gothic cathedral, enormous, yet bold in structure, and free and varied in ornamental detail.

He was the son of an advocate-general, and was to have been a lawyer himself. But he employed his youth in composing comedies, which were not at all remarkable, or essentially different from those of Garnier and Hardy. Going to Paris, he there brought out, in 1629, a better comedy, "Mélite," which met with considerable success. For the next six years he continued to write chiefly comedies, and it was not till 1635 that he produced a good tragedy, "Médée." But it was the next year, 1636, that the young poet suddenly thrust his head above the level of mediocrity. In that year he brought out the "Cid," a tragedy. It was a close imitation, in plot and details of action, of a Spanish play by De Castro, and, it may reasonably be asked, wherein consists its originality? I should say that the originality of the "Cid," and what made it mark an epoch, was the fact that in it, for the first time in French literature, a really strong intelligence, governed by a high moral character, poured itself forth, sincerely and enthusiastically in a dramatic theme.

Suddenly, on the appearance of that play, there was revealed to France the proud, pure, chivalrous heart of Corneille, and she recognized in him, though not quite immediately, her first great dramatic poet. He was, and in this play first showed himself to be, an example of one of the most admirable ideals of that age, — its ideal of elevated, dignified, eloquent conduct in love and danger. Corneille found in his own heart the central character of the "Cid," Don Rodrigue. Three years later, when he was only thirty-three years old, he produced "Horace," a tragedy founded on a familiar anecdote in Roman history, and

"Cinna," also of Roman origin. The next year he produced "Polyeucte," the fourth and last of his masterpieces; for though he lived till 1684, and wrote voluminously, he never again attained the sincerity, the youthful idealism, the fire and fervor, the sublimity, of these early works. There are many critics who consider "Polyeucte" the best of the four. But readers and playgoers generally prefer the "Cid," and, I think, with reason. "Polyeucte" is based upon the life of an early Christian martyr, and the two ideals, of Christian sacrifice and of chivalric honor, which are commingled in it are incapable of perfect fusion, for the basis of the former is humility, and of the latter pride. The "Cid" is an eloquent expression of the old chivalric idea of honor, unmixed with any other view of life, either Christian or selfish or utilitarian. It seems to have come forth in a single jet, as the French say, and is the most unified and characteristic of Corneille's tragedies. As the poet grew more critical of his own writing, and more conscious of his public, he departed farther from that high ground of generous emotion where his youthful heart poured forth the "Cid."

But if Corneille in his tragedies portrayed and idealized the social order in its heroic aspect; if he set forth royalty as an unassailable and absolute unit, and a high noble caste as deriving from royalty all its rights and all its admirable qualities; if in his sincere and stately works he blew the trumpet of praise to usher in the young king who was to be in his own person the epitome of national greatness and national completeness, — if Corneille did do all this, there was still left even in France a large mass of humanity, which, in spite of the intense centralization of the nation, could by no means be said to come within the social order as he conceived it. His plays contain no criticism of common life, — no sympathy, and not even a helpful laugh, for ordinary men and women. The people are not represented. The business and professional classes could not possibly see themselves in the grandiose characters of Corneille, — in the Horatii and Don Rodrigue, men of antique fibre and mighty-sounding antique speech. It remained for some one else than Corneille, therefore, to picture the life of France, not in general outline, as a great unified system, but in detail; not in its noblest aspects only, but also where it was excessive or ridiculous, or even merely gay and natural. It remained for some one to represent artistically, not the ideal summit of life, narrow and sheer and perhaps unattainable, to which the seventeenth century aspired, but things as they really were.

In the years when Corneille, having accomplished his reform, having completed his picture of the grand side of life, having created French tragedy, was seen to be incapable of rivalling himself, — in the early years of Corneille's long decline, the king of comedy was travelling about the country as a strolling actor. In comedy alone could the details of life which lay beneath the pompous show of absolutism be given artistic representation, — in comedy alone, and in lyric poetry, for the novel was not yet developed into an exponent of contemporary manners and morals. And although in poetry — in the fables of La Fontaine — the humble details of life were recognized and most deftly employed, the fables of La Fontaine are almost the only non-dramatic poems which that age produced in France, and even these little masterpieces are but miniatures. It required the broad, hearty laugh of Molière, his piercing eye, his resistless charm, his wide and deep experience of the ways and works of men, it required comedy, in a word, — for Molière is comedy in person, — to discover and analyze and artistically reconstruct the real France.

Molière's rise to public view was made possible by the direct exercise of royal favor, and is an illustration of what good may sometimes come of benevolent absolutism. In a republic, or under a government by parliament, he might have been borne down by popular conservatism or the jealousy of the great. But in personal alliance with an enlightened despot he was enabled to be fairly independent of the people, — for short periods only, of course, for the comedian after all must draw his very life from the people, — and to smile at the rage of dukes and marquises. We are so accustomed to think of liberty as the mother of the arts, that it is hard for us to realize how much good has often come to literature from the patronage of tyrants, — a selfish patronage, perhaps, but often effective.

There is no name in French literature at all comparable with that of Molière. He is, in fact, the one world-genius which the

French race has produced. La Fontaine, I think it is fair to say, comes second; but to enjoy him one must needs be versed, not only in the French language, but in the French heart. His very delicacy of flavor is a bar to perfect comprehension, and therefore to perfect enjoyment by foreigners. And even if an apt and sympathetic student of La Fontaine should translate him well, even if all the world could appreciate him as do the best French minds, he would still come short of being a universal poet, like Chaucer and Schiller, because he lacks their "high seriousness," and because French verse is not so good a medium for poetic expression as English or German verse. There is no name in the older French literature except La Fontaine's which for world-wide influence can be for a moment considered to rival Molière's. And there has been no creator of comedy except Shakespeare worthy to sit beside Molière with the Athenians, Aristophanes and Menander, and the Romans, Plautus and Terence.

Such a genius is personal, and might be supposed to enter the world as meteors flash through our earth's enveloping atmosphere, unannounced, and independent of contemporary needs. It is true that under any circumstances, in any country, and at any time, Molière would probably have observed and penetrated to the roots of human conduct, and would have been an excellent imitator. But the facts in his life tell a much less simple story; and they are very interesting. They show how the soil and air of a highly organized society under an absolute monarch were precisely what this talented comedian required to develop into a powerful genius. Let us look at these facts. The dates themselves are eloquent. Molière was born in Paris in 1622, and went on the stage in 1646, when twenty-four years old. He organized a company, with which he travelled for twelve years among the country towns and minor cities of France. To act in the provinces alone was no great career in those days, any more than it is now. Nor was it at all remarkable for a manager to write comedies and farces for his troupe. So that although by the end of these twelve years Molière had composed no small number of pieces and performed in them in many places, he had done nothing notable, and was considered to have achieved only an ordinary, honorable success when he found himself rich and confident and popular enough to come to Paris in 1658 and set up a theatre. His first hall was in the Petit-Bourbon Palace, near the Louvre, but he presently removed to the Palais Royal.

The breath of the capital at once freed his hitherto confined activities. The old order was changing. Men were already wearying of the fashions and manners that had prevailed under Richelieu and Mazarin, and wishing the young king would assert himself. Molière's first great comedy, which was also the first great dramatic study of French manners ever written, "Les Précieuses ridicules," was produced in 1659, its author taking the leading rôle, that of Mascarille. Consciously, and as if aware that he was allying himself with the new spirit of the times, as represented in the king, Molière ridiculed in this play the affectation, the inflated language, the exaggerated manners, the æsthetic pedantry, of the age. Never after Louis XIV. began to rule in person would it be possible for courtiers to indulge in such nonsense. The etiquette of his court was to be complicated and severe, and in many ways artificial, but it was not to be absurd. Molière seems to have divined this, and "Les Précieuses ridicules" was a warning to blue-stockings and dandies that they must learn to speak French, and no longer call a mirror the counsellor of the graces, or a chair the commodity of conversation.

"Les Précieuses ridicules" was a criticism of contemporary life, and could never have been created outside of the capital, or far from the palace of that king who was known to be the personification of good sense and good taste. It was followed by other comedies, not all of them so manifestly full of tendency. In fact, some are farces, like "Sganarelle," not differing essentially from those with which Molière had been wont to amuse provincial audiences. But in 1665 he produced a long and remarkable comedy of quite another sort, called "Don Juan" or the "Festin de Pierre." The daredevil character of the principal personage brought down on Molière the censure of the unco guid. He was attacked for impiety, and it looked at one moment as if the police would have to withdraw his privilege of managing a theatre. It was at this juncture, 't is worth our while to notice, that the king silenced calumny and encouraged the brave comedian by pensioning both him and his troupe. "Don Juan" is not a comedy of contemporary manners, but a romantic comedy, something very rare in French literature. It was the only one Molière wrote, and he was not even imitated in this type of writing, down to Alfred de Musset. Shakespeare is the magician who has shown us what romantic comedy may be by the "Midsummer Night's Dream," by "As You Like It," by "A Winter's Tale." Those who love Molière and are glad to do homage to his personal genius prize this play as exhibiting an otherwise only latent power, the power of warm romantic imagination.

Next year came the most subtle, the most profound, the most poetical of all French dramas, whether of tragedies or comedies. It is usually called a comedy, but if the sadness of deceived love and the seriousness of a noble heart have in them aught of tragic grandeur, then the "Misanthrope" of Molière is as much a tragedy as "King Lear" or "Hamlet." It is a touching protest against the insincerity of ordinary social relations, against trifling in love, against cynicism and conventional lying. The hero is a plain-spoken, just man, who looks upon the world with childlike good faith, and tells the truth unfalteringly. His disenchantment, his amazement at the falseness of men, and especially of women, and his true-hearted constancy, nevertheless, to what he believes is right, make him a figure as pathetic as he is noble. The play is thought to be autobiographical, in so far at least as it relates an unhappy love affair. We know that Molière's marriage was most unfortunate, and his wife unworthy of him.

The "Misanthrope" was followed by "Tartufe," a daring criticism of religious hypocrisy; and once more the royal favor had to be exerted to protect Molière from the fury of Jesuits and fools. Among his later pieces, "L'Avare" is a thorough study of the character of the miser, taken as a type; "Le Bourgeois Gentilhomme," a farcical satire on men of the middle class who ape the manners of the nobility; "Les Femmes savantes," a protest against the new education of women; "Le Malade imaginaire," a clever hit at doctors.

In all Molière's works written after his establishment in Paris we find the same zeal for the more natural and dignified manners favored by Louis XIV., as opposed to the exaggerated fashions of an earlier time. The atmosphere of most of his plays written after 1658 is that of the court. He had but to transfer to his stage the marquises and countesses whom he found acting their parts in the Louvre, and behold, he gave us comedy! The dialogue in the more important of his plays is courtly. We have here not simply the ridiculous side of court life, but much that is serious, much that is beautiful. And his work is all interesting and all truly representative. But throughout, there is also a revelation of Molière's personality. It is immensely attractive. We learn, first of all, his fondness for whatever is natural. He loves good, simple people. He loves good, simple poetry. He has a fine scorn of pretence and sham. A hundred passages could be quoted to illustrate his hatred of hypocrisy. He here and there alludes gracefully to the favor the king had shown him, and pays homage to the king's successes; but he never stoops to flattery, and it is like one potentate saluting another. The pathos of his end is none the less because mingled with irony. Although sick unto death, he went manfully on the stage lest the poor men and women in his employment should suffer for want of work if he closed his theatre, and it was while acting the "Malade imaginaire," a satire on his enemies the doctors, that he suffered a mortal seizure, in 1673. No gayer, gentler, kinder man ever graced the stage. No eye was ever so sharp to discover human weakness, no heart more quick to excuse it. Wherever men read or listen to Molière, there laughter is, — the freest, healthiest, most irrepressible laughter, — but there rises in us a sad wonder, too, at the foibles of men and women; and the mind is mellowed by reflecting on human sorrow wreathed in smiles, and human goodness inextricably mingled with wickedness and folly.

'T was in 1673, the year of Molière's death, that Racine produced "Mithridate," one of his first great tragedies. He had been at court for some years, having come to public notice and royal favor by an ode on the occasion of the king's wedding. But the grand Corneille was still before the world, and Racine, young and gentle, developed slowly. As the king's reign reached the climax of its greatness, however, in the notable decade of political and social power between 1673 and 1683, Racine grew equal to the times, and wrote his "Iphigénie" and his "Phèdre." Offended by some adverse criticism of the latter, and affected also by religious scruples against working for the stage, he suddenly withdrew from the praises of the world, and devoted himself to his family, to theological and poetical studies, and to his duties as court historian. When he issued from retirement, twelve years later, it was in response to a demand of Madame de Maintenon that he should write a tragedy for the school for young ladies at Saint Cyr which was under her patronage. He chose the story of Esther, from the Old Testament, and when the wonderful success of his attempt drew from him another, two years later, he again selected a biblical theme, and wrote "Athalie." Racine is a better illustration than either Corneille or Molière of what the spirit of the times could do. His personality was not so strong as theirs, and he was young and susceptible in that decade when the spirit of absolutism in a highly organized society had more completely expressed itself. And by that time Molière was dead, and Corneille too old to be inspired by the new ideals. Racine's tragedies are consequently the most typical glories of the classical French drama. For regularity and finish, for scrupulous avoidance of whatever savors of common life and common speech, they are unmatched even by Corneille. Their versification is perhaps the smoothest and most musical in all French literature. They excel as much in what they are not as in what they are. To the French mind, ever striving after distinctness and intellectual completeness within the bounds of common sense, and easily shocked by rude emphasis or unbalanced power, Racine is synonymous with perfection.

Voltaire, the most assiduous and admiring student of Racine, respected his achievements more, probably, than those of any other man who ever lived. We can excuse the national bias when it leads even Voltaire to worship, though it is hard to realize that such a thorough scholar of English as Voltaire was, and such a lover of the drama, could have called Shakespeare "a drunken savage, without the smallest spark of good taste, and without the least acquaintance with the rules." Listen to Racine at his best, and you may fancy you see a stately company of noble lords and ladies winding through the mazes of an ancient minuet, with delicate precision and admired restraint. But we who have been used to English speech and English poetry are compelled to feel that this is very artificial and constrained, when our ears catch sound of the mighty rushing wind which is the voice of Shakespeare.

But Shakespeare in connection with French literature is all modern. He is a romantic, and romanticism in France is of the nineteenth century. And this reminds us that in speaking of Racine's latest plays, written at the command of the royal mistress-wife, we have crossed the divide in French history. Classicism and unchallenged absolutism we have seen ascending the vast slope together, to a summit of joint perfection, reached when Louis XIV. was in his prime. By 1683 the classical French drama was a thing accomplished. Molière was dead, Corneille about to die, and Racine had done his life-work, all but his last two pieces. Human presumption and ingenuity, the power and pride of a victorious monarch, had held together and brought to this high pass the most completely organized society in the world. Henceforth this company was doomed to go downhill, to separate at the partings of the ways, and to dissolve finally in helpless disunion. The song they chanted, the music of their three great artists, was to endure. It is still the noblest thing that remains of all that age of grandeur.

If we would behold that splendid and conspicuous company as it stands, united and triumphant, on the summit of attainment in 1683, it must be with a brief and final glance For the descent into ruin is sharp. One false step after another scatters and thins the bewildered band. The disintegration of French society began with the death of the queen in 1683, which removed the greatest obstacle to the legitimation of the bastard princes. In 1684 the king secretly married Madame de Maintenon, thus putting himself under the control of a bigoted woman whose conscience was directed by Jesuit confessors. Their hand is seen the next year in the revocation of the Edict of Nantes, by which half a million Protestants were driven from France to rival countries, and in the twenty years of persecution for religion, which began immediately in the South. These atrocities helped to consolidate Europe against the king who had now become a dangerous despot; and the coalition of hostile powers was formed in 1686. After some years of costly victories, even the French arms began to fail, and France suffered terrible defeats, at Blenheim in 1704, at Ramillies in 1706, at Malplaquet in 1709. In 1711 the hand of God fell heavily upon the king's lineage, so that it seemed as if, in Dante's words, a just judgment, novel, and visible to all men, fell from the stars upon his blood; for in that year died his only legitimate son, and next year died that son's son, the Duke of Burgundy, and his young and lovely wife. A twelvemonth later he lost Newfoundland and Nova Scotia, and yet the obstinate old king persisted in religious persecution, breaking up the best schools in France because they were taught by the Port Royal reformers, and forcing his clergy to sign the bull Unigenitus, which condemned the Jansenists. When he died, in 1715, multitudes made holiday, and mockery arose along the line of his funeral journey. The Revolution had begun. It is still going on, though more than two centuries have elapsed since its beginning.

What is the French Revolution? It is,

I think, first of all a conviction that social perfection has never been attained, even in the great reign of Louis XIV. And it is, secondly, a confidence that human nature is able, by the Reason, to work out a state of social perfection, some day and somehow, — the idea of a conscious, rational social evolution. We have not yet seen the whole course of the French Revolution completed. There are still unsatisfied theorists at work on the banks of the Seine, restlessly urging untried issues. But so far as the Revolution has proceeded, we may see in it two lines of effort, — the line of protest against the past and the line of hopeful search into the future, the line of analysis and the line of synthesis, the line of destruction and the line of reconstruction. Along the former line we see the labors of Voltaire; along the latter are the remains of Rousseau's ideal fabrics. Along the one line we have the barricades and the guillotine, the revolts of 1789, 1830, 1848, and 1871; along the other we have the successive constitutions under which France has existed during the last eleven decades.

And not alone in politics was the age of Louis XIV. followed by an age of revolution. In philosophy and in art the same changes have occurred. The modern literature of France is not classical, but romantic. It is a literature of experiment, indeed often of protest. There is perpetual war among the various schools of poetry and fiction. Great reputations decline as rapidly as they are made. Modern French works are called masterpieces for a day, and then forgotten. Fortunate are we, then, to have still something upon which the seal of universal approval has been set, something forever fair and serenely secure, something classical, in a word. What matters it to us that the old society has crumbled, in the midst of which this beautiful thing, the classical French drama, was produced? That social system was corrupt. The great king ruled, not by divine right, as he supposed, but by craft and oppression. King and social system deserved their downfall, but the drama they helped to form is a thing of beauty and shall endure. We are told that Samson, after he had killed a lion in the vineyards of Timnath, going back that way, "turned aside to see the carcass of the lion; and, behold, there was a swarm of bees, and honey, in the carcass of the lion. And he took thereof in his hands, and went on, eating, and came to his father and mother, and they did eat; but he told not them that he had taken the honey out of the carcass of the lion."

THE REVOLUTIONARY ANALYSIS

SAINT-SIMON AND MONTESQUIEU

THE REVOLUTIONARY ANALYSIS

SAINT-SIMON AND MONTESQUIEU

THE French Revolution may properly be said to have begun in the closing years of the seventeenth century. It was then that the system of absolutism attained completion, then also that its limitations of barrenness and hard brutality were disclosed. Outraged nature called aloud for revenge. Frenchmen asked themselves whether they were receiving an adequate return for their expenditure of blood and treasure, and for the surrender to the Crown of every sort of temporal advantage, and to the Church of all spiritual independence. For a long time at first criticism was uttered with bated breath, during the last thirty years of Louis XIVth's life. But under the Regency clearer voices arose and boldly compared France with happier lands enjoying rational laws. The import of these protests was unsuspected by the government and unrealized even by their authors, who nearly all belonged, in fact, to the privileged classes. Men were hardly conscious of a changed relation. But after the lapse of two hundred years it is possible for us to discern a distinct alteration of feeling, dating from about 1685. It is discoverable first in private letters and secret memoirs, where we remark an unwonted freedom of speech concerning the corruption of the court, a ridicule of the old king which would have shocked the previous generation, and a reluctant presentiment of national defeat at the hands of England and her allies. Saint-Simon particularly made a tremendous outcry against the legitimation of the bastard princes, a measure which he rightly considered fatal to the position of the old feudal nobility.

But except for these faint or incoherent protests, which may, it is true, be regarded as the beginnings of the Revolutionary propaganda, there could be nothing more unified, more characteristic and consistent, than French literature in the reign of Louis XIV. It is a well-nigh perfect harmony. The instruments, you will say, are of few kinds, as in an orchestra of Haydn's day. The music is often shallow. But it is certainly refined and well concerted, except for this one discordant note. During the seventy-two years of Louis XIVth's reign, from 1643 to 1715, there were developed a type and a body of literature so peculiarly French and so excellent that this, together with the succeeding time of imitation, has by common consent been called the classical period.

The influence of the king is manifest in all this work, and withal a national spirit pervades it. The monarchy gave to the world nothing else half so fine, or that has endured half so long, as the classical French literature. It was fostered by royal patronage and possesses royal worth. It has the great virtue of distinction, a virtue not foreign to courts, even in their decay. It is dignified and simple. It is clear and graceful. For public life under Louis XIV., despite its inward rottenness, and in spite also of its brutal abuse of force, was in the main characterized by respect for whatsoever was of good report. Literature was deliberately and intelligently cultivated as one of the most creditable ornaments of the throne. If the result was artificial, it was thoroughly artistic; that is, it testified to great industry guided by good taste. It is indeed worthy of the throne, representing nobly the throne's stability, magnificence, and haughty elevation. And it is almost as direct a product of the monarch's power as were the army, or the foreign policy, or the court etiquette.

This may be said without prejudice to the independent merit of the works of Corneille and Pascal, of Molière and La Fontaine, of Racine and La Bruyère, of Fénelon and Bossuet. If these great men were caught in the resistless currents of destiny and made to revolve around one central fact, and that the terrible and iniquitous fact of absolutism in Church and State, we should not complain, but rather rejoice that their native wit and manliness preserved them from indecent subjection. It is remarkable what individuality they display, though all their writings are stamped with the seal of royal authority. Their work is limited; but it is select. It is not always broadly human; but it has the good qualities of an aristocracy, — it is marked by dignity, reserve, wit, fineness, form.

The first voices of protest were raised against political corruption only. The ravages of unnecessary warfare and of boundless extravagance could not but be immediately felt, though the loss of religious and social integrity might be for a while unrealized.

But even this suspension of sentence was exhausted before the old king's death. The worst condemnation of his despotic system is in the fact that when the leading men died who had made his reign illustrious, none were left to fill their places. Confining our attention to literature, we see that only two of the great writers of his era, Massillon and Saint-Simon, survived the year 1715; so short-lived and so barren of offspring was the boasted culture of the golden age. However vigorous and beautiful, it was a parasitic growth. It developed, not from popular enlightenment nor the discipline of the national conscience, but from the narrow, the exclusive, the unnatural conditions of absolutism.

When Louis XIV., through darkening years of political and domestic loss, reached the limit where flattery can no longer deceive and patronage no longer influence, if he could have looked about him with discerning eyes he must have seen that he stood alone. The poets and philosophers who gave charm and depth to life in the early years of his reign were silent. The serene, consoling voices of his great prelates, promising heavenly approval, were now but hollow echoes, mocking at reality. The generals and financiers, the ministers of state, the architects, the masters of ceremonies, who had shared his glory and helped him ruin France, had nearly all been consigned to more or less dishonored graves. Their successors who surrounded him were a degenerate race. The fathers had eaten sour grapes, and the children's teeth were set on edge. No revival of manhood could be expected from them. And if with the clairvoyance of the dying his gaze penetrated the future, he must have seen that not only was the great chapter in French literature finished and the peculiar culture of his age outworn, but that the new time would be hostile to the old. His injustice to the people was to be atoned for by a political revolution, which had begun already. The attacks he had made on religious and civil freedom were to deprive France, for many generations, of moral strength and spiritual vigor. He left to his country a heritage of isolation, poverty, and false political theories. England had founded her colonial empire and her commerical supremacy on the ruins of his costly schemes of conquest. The barbarities he had authorized or permitted against the Rhine provinces were to make Germany the hereditary foe of France. Holland and Spain, the extremes of the continental system, he had made equally his foes, when one or the other might have been his ally.

The one imperishable and precious treasure of his reign, which should be the nation's pride forevermore, and of which no revolution, no social decay, no foreign enemy could diminish the value, was its literature. The vein apparently was worked out; but a great accumulation was already made, solid, pure, unchangeable. To us both facts are important: that the literature of the age of Louis XIV. is truly great and truly typical of what was best in seventeenth-century France, and that its production terminated with astonishing sharpness.

It is singular that the most notable survivor, and except Massillon the only great writer to survive,—it is singular that the solitary figure which stands firmly outlined against the lowering sky amid all this wreckage, is Saint-Simon, because he is not properly of Louis XIVth's time at all. He voyaged through its later part and recorded the truth concerning it as no one else dared do. But the reason is that he saw with the eyes of one who was not of that world. He was the last defender of feudalism, which was to him an ideal system. He was attached to it by principle, undoubtedly, but also by self-interest. As a great hereditary nobleman, a duke and peer, he saw himself robbed of honor and influence by the assumptions of the monarchy. He saw the Crown strengthening itself by encroaching on the aristocracy, and the latter losing its old political ambition for the sake of the wealth connected with court offices and favors. He realized that Louis XIV. was completing the work begun by Louis XI., and reducing the old active aristocracy to a mere disfranchised, wealthy class, entirely dependent upon royal favor and liable to be reduced in the future to the level of the populace.

These considerations, combined with personal resentment of ill-treatment, made Saint-Simon the unacknowledged defender of his order, which was so lost to self-respect that it ridiculed him for his pains. He remained tenacious of his class privileges and reverenced his own name. But it was a losing fight. He was slow to learn that the nobility was no longer a wheel in the machine of government. He looked back with regret to the days of Saint Louis, when the barons of France were but little lower than the king. Or perhaps he contemplated with envy the growth of party government in England, where an aristocracy of great political vitality was steadily limiting the royal power by a constitution more inviolable than the throne itself. But it was vain to hope for a revival or transformation of feudalism now, in France.

So we may say that in one sense Saint-Simon was a representative of an older age than the age of Louis XIV. His character, as well as his political aspirations, allied him to the past. He was of sterner stuff than his contemporaries. Although a rigid Catholic, he was something of a Puritan, and in that respect more like the writers of his youth than those of his later age. He was as rude and bluff, considering his circumstances, as any old partisan of the Wars of Religion in the days of Henri IV. In another sense, however, Saint-Simon was a prophet of things new and the first man of the eighteenth century. The same aloofness that made him seem old-fashioned, his virtual isolation in the midst of a court which he condemned, his occasional exile from the royal presence, gave him his distinguishing faculty of independent vision and plain speech. He was often too violently swayed by passion to see things as they really were; but the eyes he saw with were at least his own, and he was a man. This duke and peer, so tenacious of the prerogatives of his order, would have been surprised to be called a revolutionary writer, yet his memoirs are the earliest and no small contribution to the great literature of protest which represents at least three-fourths of eighteenth-century French thought.

Louis de Rouvroy, Duc de Saint-Simon, was born in 1675 of an ancient family which traced its lineage back to Charlemagne. He died in 1755. Of his father Sainte-Beuve says: "If I had to define in two words Saint-Simon's father, I should say that he was a favorite, but not a courtier, for he had a sense of honor and a temper." The son inherited both, adding to them a pronounced literary instinct of most uncommon quality. In 1693, after the battle of Neerwinden, in which he served as an officer of the Royal Roussillon regiment, he sent to his mother a graphic account of the campaign. The next year, he began systematically to write his memoirs, while still in the army. In 1694, the famous Duc de Luxembourg, puffed up by his victories in these wars, "thought himself strong enough to rise from the eighteenth rank, which he held among the peers, to the second." Sixteen dukes and peers, Saint-Simon the most eager of them all, protested against this assault on their prerogatives. Henceforth the memoirs are colored throughout by a sense of injustice and a determination to resist encroachments upon his order or his personal rights. Virtuous, pious in a narrow but real sense, animated even in youth by an old man's reverence for the past and for ancient forms of procedure, stubbornly jealous of his title, and acquainted with the family history of all the French nobility and most of the hangers-on at court, he was ill fitted to succeed there, but admirably prepared to observe and record the truth. Making every allowance for the bitterness of his invective and his constant bias, which is frankly disclosed, Saint-Simon is yet the capital authority for the history of court life in France from 1692 to 1723. It is doubtful if his passion really invalidates, in any essential respect, his documentary value.

Passion, not so much poetic as personal, informs his pages. They glow with intense heat. The hurrying phrases crowd each other like panting horses in a race. As Nisard pithily says, " Saint-Simon is at the same time cumbersome and full of rushing power; he is a torrent which appears embarassed by the débris it floats, but sweeps none the less swiftly on." His abundance is only equalled by the breathless vehemence of his purpose. From austere judgments on questions of law he turns deftly to light anecdotes. Whatever comes uppermost in his mind is made to serve his turn. Elaborate portraits are mingled with pregnant insinuations conveyed in a brief phrase. As nothing escaped his eye, so he shrinks from no detail and spares no susceptibilities. Hot resentment of injury alternates with tumultuous, stammering, stamping exultation over his enemies' defeat, even in the most trifling matters. The vastness of the cupidities engaged in these questions of precedence makes us forget the pettiness of the disputes, as Nisard again remarks. The memoirs of Saint-Simon would be a boon to a man in solitary confinement or cast away on a desert island, for they quickly draw around one a narrow, but distinct and unbroken, horizon, and fill the circumscribed space with a rich abundance of varied and highly developed human beings, moved by complicated and restless passions, and interacting in a way both dramatic and real.

As becomes a duke and peer, and it might be added, as becomes a great master of language, Saint-Simon is superior to the plebeian restrictions of grammar. With a paragraph, a phrase, a word, he summons from happy oblivion and hangs up in the picture-gallery of immortal condemnation the sycophants and parasites who stole by crawling what he scorned to stoop for, though it was his own. The indubitable literary success of his writings is a proof, if any be needed, that an intensely passionate expression of abundant knowledge is three-fourths of a great style.

His power of reproduction in words is superb. He could reproduce so well because he remembered precisely. He remembered precisely because he saw with the vividness of keen personal feeling. Hence the style of the memoirs is a sufficient witness to their truthfulness. They possess us in detail with the record of more than one day at court, from the king's putting on his shirt and saying his morning prayer, to the evening card-party, lighted by we know just how many candles, and followed by the *grand* and the *petit coucher*. Accounts of what happened in the long hours between are given with the fulness of stenographic reports, but in the richly colored language of a great artist. We see the king and Madame de Maintenon at Mass, then seated together at the council-table. We hear courtiers having an audience; we read their satisfaction or disappointment on their faces, and catch their whispered asides as they bow themselves out of the Presence. We walk at a respectful distance behind the Monarch as he strolls in the afternoon sunlight beside his fish-ponds at Versailles, and travel in due order behind his ponderous coach on the royal progresses.

It must not be supposed that Saint-Simon paints these scenes with deliberate artistic purpose. This, like a too careful observance of grammatical rules, would have been beneath his dignity. They are not descriptive, but narrative; all the more wonderful art for that reason, of course, like the highest dramatic poetry, but art without effort.

Saint-Simon's representation of court life under Louis XIV., while more interesting than the comparatively colorless eulogy of Voltaire, is on the whole unfavorable. No one acquainted with Saint-Simon can maintain, if anybody still does maintain, a worshipful attitude towards the Grand Monarch. Yet some allowance must be made for personal disappointment. The king disapproved, naturally, of the young hot-head who was known to be taking notes. Doubtless Saint-Simon was a vehement talker. Doubtless he vented his resentment, not only on paper, after retiring from the day's occupations to the privacy of his study, but openly in conversation. We know, in fact, from his own inimitable account of the interview, that the old king reprimanded him once for the freedom of his expressions.

Of course, Saint-Simon never dreamed of what we should term political progress, in the direction of liberal government. His ideal lay in the past, and was the feudal system, wherein royal prerogative was limited by equally inviolable baronial rights. For him the people had no political existence. He was far from realizing that feudalism could never return. He did dimly foresee that by breaking down the independence of the nobility royalty would be left face to face with the voiceless masses; but that the masses should ever stir into political activity we have no evidence of his having even surmised. He was revolutionary only in that he dared to see, and in an unsystematic way to criticise. Little did he know that in the existing stage of political evolution, movement could be only in one direction, and that to breathe was to precipitate an avalanche.

It is revolutionary thought and revolutionary writing which must almost exclusively engage the attention of any one dealing with the history of French literature during the eighteenth century. We may go further, and say during the eighteenth and nineteenth centuries. Modern French literature, no less than modern French political history, is a record of swiftly varying temperatures, hallucinations beautiful or vile, periods of exhaustion alternating with outbursts of abnormal energy, now a noble exaltation, now a blind, brutal spasm. The study of modern French literature, and by modern I mean to include both the last centuries, seems at times to be largely a pathological study. It is the study of a national mind which seems at times not altogether sane. We have left the classical period, serenely beautiful, serenely strong, and entered a period of unrest and disorder. Henceforth we shall observe much to disquiet us if we possess any feeling for the classic type, much to confuse our notions of what art is and what it should and can express. Our attention will be drawn by her literature to all points of the complicated problem of France's destiny. We shall be forced to contemplate her social ills, her political strifes, her moral weaknesses. We shall witness a bewildering confusion of ideals, forms, and systems. We shall perhaps fancy we detect a falling off in vigor, a loss of balance, and in recent years an appalling decline. Are these phenomena symptoms of a real disease, or are they but the pangs of birth and growth? A great hope has animated and still animates the on-lookers, — a hope that out of many changes the Best may yet emerge. It is this sense of witnessing a crisis, in which the incomplete is striving for perfection, that lends peculiar fascination to the study of revolutionary eras. In any case, whether the ultimate issue be life or death, the literature of modern France is alive in every part, and full of strange surprises.

The structural perfection of the system which absolutism had created was the very thing that rendered impossible any change short of revolution. From its very completeness it was incapable of adaptation. For example, the fact that the sale of public offices was normal made all members of the office-holding class rich, contented, dependent on one another, and independent of the people at large. The government was a close corporation, firmly centralized, conveniently managed, almost automatic. Its affairs could be controlled quietly. No constitution, no political parties, no elections, no parliament, no debates, no public meetings rallied and excited general opinion. It was less difficult for the French government to declare war than for the English government to pension a doorkeeper. The public was seldom called upon to awake from its lethargy to consider troublesome questions. There may well, then, have been some difficulty in persuading the comfortable bourgeois class that they were not well governed, and immense difficulty in forcing their rulers to change the smallest detail of the system.

Orderly reformation was impossible not

only for these reasons, but because of the poverty and ignorance of the bread-producing and tax-paying peasantry, out of whom had been starved all that vigor which might have armed a French Wiclif or Wat Tyler, a French Luther or Lincoln. If it be difficult to think of the French peasantry of that age, or even the social stratum next above the peasantry, as putting forth such fruit, and if the parallel seem therefore inexact, this really does but illuminate the situation. The impossibility of quiet, slow reform was doubled by the fact that the tyranny itself was double. It was not only political, but religious. Inseparably bound up in the theory of royal supremacy was the dogma of the inerrancy of the Church. Temporal and spiritual authority were under mutual obligations. Their united weight was irresistible. The faintest whisper of political dissent was regarded as an heretical outcry. The mildest forms of religious independence were liable to be crushed out by civil power. This was a matter, too, of still more intimate character, for every political reformer had first to struggle with his own conscience, realizing that he must give up reform or lose his religious equilibrium. And in any case, when men did dare to inquire what caused the enfeeblement of the nation and their own misery, they saw that even should the monarchy abate its claims and release its pressure, the Church would still remain, a crushing load on property, law, and mind.

The Huguenots, who might have led their countrymen to face this problem, and whose ancestors, indeed, once had heroically faced it, were now in exile or silenced by the revocation of the Edict of Nantes. By permitting the Jesuits to break up the Port Royal schools, Louis XIV. had stifled another intelligent party from which leaders might have arisen. By the dragonnades of the Cévennes he had stilled the inarticulate murmur of the peasant and mountaineer. Thus, with no hope of organic reform, there was needed a cataclysm, a tidal wave, an earthquake. Yet the upheaval was to be prepared slowly. The process of preparation was to be a gradual indoctrination. It was to work from above downward. It was to be intellectual. No other process was possible, because any other would have been detected and stopped. A scholar of noble blood, and moving in the highest circles, might teach almost openly what a man without these advantages would scarce be permitted to think. It was a task for the philosopher, rather than the practical man, for the scholarly critic, rather than the active politician.

This great responsibility was laid first of all upon a few men of letters. Never, probably, in the history of the world, did literature perform such an important political task. And it is scarcely an exaggeration to say that to this work French literature of the eighteenth century was entirely devoted. If literature thus achieved a triumph in politics, it was at no small sacrifice, for in being so absorbed in public life it lost grandeur, variety, and charm. Instead of Pascal's high speculations on divine and human nature, abstract and free from bias, we find the political pamphlet, written to persuade, and brimful of "tendencies." Instead of the genial La Fontaine, instilling wisdom by a nudge or a smile, like a good-natured fellow-traveller on life's way, we find the pedantic insistence of the Encyclopedists. From one end of the century to the other, literature written simply to please is almost wanting. Controversial intentions pervade even most of the professedly belletristic writing. Poetry suffers most. Indeed it may be questioned whether a line of real poetry was written in all that period, down to André de Chénier, just before its close. Much excellent work was done in comedy, but it is worthy of remark that "Le Mariage de Figaro," the most notable dramatic success of the century, was political in fundamental conception and in effect. In tragedy, Voltaire strove to continue the classical tradition, writing plays which conform rigidly to the type as perfected by Racine. But they are barren of true poetry. They are clever and correct, but neither grand nor touching. Eloquent prose is wanting also, except in Rousseau and his followers. After Massillon there were no great literary preachers, — no Bossuets or Fénelons of the eighteenth century. The age was rich, however, in the kinds of literary success which require less genius, and for which intelligence and political aspiration suffice. Letter-writing and memoir-writing especially attained perfection. The prose style of Voltaire, Madame du Deffand, Vauvenargues, and their contemporaries in the early half of the century, though deficient in eloquence and pathos, is unequalled as a means of ordinary social intercourse.

Rousseau, at first alone, and seconded only

late in his life by the slowly kindling enthusiasm of a new school, imparts a touch of poetic fire to French thought in the latter half of the century. To complete our general view of the eighteenth century in France, it would be necessary to consider the revolutionary synthesis, to observe how the disintegrating work of Voltaire and the Encyclopedists was followed by the constructive work of the Genevan dreamer. No systematic understanding of the subject is possible without an appreciation of his place as the prophet of that age, who built for later times. The singular fascination of the man, the mysterious beginning and end of his career, the loneliness of his high merits, the unusual circumstances and time of life when they appeared, the elemental forces which he fingered with elemental genius, the passion he stirred, and finally the lasting and wide-reaching results of his work, are topics which would naturally occupy the second half of any thorough survey of that era. He gives color to a period of French literature that but for him and Saint-Simon might seem to lack the glow of imagination.

Except Buffon, there is no great eighteenth-century French author whose works are not more or less charged with revolutionary lightning. And these men were in most cases conscious of their mission. They were nearly all filled with a common spirit of reform, which was a bond among themselves and a distinction. Of course there were others who wrote without any political ambition, but even their books have a strong revolutionary tendency, as, for example, the Abbé Prévost's celebrated novel, "Manon Lescaut." It is evident from a glance at eighteenth-century French literature that the earlier writers, with Voltaire as their central figure, were devoted mainly to the task of destroying the existing system, and that the later company, inspired by Rousseau, were constructors, dreamers of ideal commonwealths, and founders, to some extent, of modern society. I think we shall not be making one of those excessively sweeping generalizations which are so dangerous in literary study, but shall be simplifying the matter in a legitimate way, if we keep in mind these preliminary conclusions: that French literature of the eighteenth century is mainly political, that it is revolutionary, and that it is in part analytic and in part synthetic.

SAINT-SIMON AND MONTESQUIEU

Montesquieu, the first great French writer belonging to the eighteenth century, except Saint-Simon, is the prototype of all who followed him. He contains in germ the analysis and the synthesis. He was the forerunner of Voltaire, and even more certainly of Rousseau. It is remarkable how much can now be discerned in him that we find more fully developed in the next generation. Fortunately for his peace, Montesquieu's genius was not fully appreciated in his lifetime. It is doubtful whether posterity also has not underestimated him. Though not so potent, he is perhaps a finer spirit than Voltaire, and in the line of political speculation a greater writer. His prose suffers little by comparison with Voltaire's. Indeed, in some respects it rather gains, because it has certain graces which Voltaire's style lacks. There is no hardness, crudity, or haste in Montesquieu. He is always elegant, and even leisurely, seeking to produce a cumulative and permanent effect. His ambition is always artistic completeness. In this he reminds us constantly of the writers of the preceding reign. It is a great achievement to have been in spirit a forerunner of the new era, while preserving in form the superior finish of the older and more gracious generation. If he yet leaves us cold, if he fails to enthrone himself in our affections or to stir our enthusiasm, he shares in this the fate of every other eighteenth-century French writer except Saint-Simon and Rousseau.

The story of his life is very simple, and his principal works, which are only three in number, may be mentioned in a few words. Charles de Secondat, Baron de la Brède et de Montesquieu, was born at the castle of La Brède, near Bordeaux, in 1689, of a noble family of Guyenne, and died in 1755. He received a sound classical education, and through family influence and his own abilities acquired a high standing in the law courts of Bordeaux, becoming president-judge in 1716, at the age of twenty-seven. His interest in literature and science found expression in the meetings of the young Academy of Bordeaux. He was of the opinion that literature could not be well cultivated except in great capitals, where many men of genius might afford the needed mutual stimulus; but that provincial academies could render valuable aid to science, by collecting data and performing experiments.

In 1721, he published, anonymously, and

only in foreign cities, Cologne and Amsterdam, two little volumes purporting to contain the letters written home by two Persians travelling in France. Paris is as strange to them as Ispahan would be to a European. They are interested in all such things as modes of travel, hotels, architecture, dress, and food, which might be expected to differ in various countries. They are astonished at the even greater dissimilarity in matters which might be supposed to differ less, such as religion, law, government, marriage relations, and education. They are amused by the sharper and more puzzling contrast in minor things, affairs of mere convention, such as social etiquette. The "Lettres persanes" are vastly entertaining, and must have been more so when they first appeared. One can enjoy them for their own sake, for their fine observations, their subtle irony, their urbane style. It is not and was not necessary to see in them a serious attack on the institutions of Montesquieu's time. It was possible to regard them as a good-natured, genial criticism, and the government, after some hesitation, chose to take this view. But when we think of the serious, thoroughgoing work their author afterwards performed, it seems likely he intended the "Lettres persanes" to mean all they now appear to imply. Whatever diversity of opinion might exist as to their political import, their literary value received prompt acknowledgment, and after some objections on the part of Louis XV. and his ministers had been cleared away, Montesquieu was admitted to the Académie française, in January, 1728.

He had already begun to collect material for other works in what we should now term comparative social science and comparative jurisprudence, and felt that he ought to see other countries. He set out, in April, 1728, in company with the English ambassador to Vienna, lived there a while, travelled in Hungary and Germany, spent a considerable time in Italy, turned northward again, and stayed in the Low Countries till October, 1729, when he passed over to England. Here he remained two years. He was the guest of Lord Chesterfield, was received at court by George II., and became a member of the Royal Society. He saw Sir Robert Walpole, Swift, and Pope. A mighty spirit of progress prevailed in England at that time. She was the home of liberty and of ideas. The supremacy of reason was loudly asserted. And yet, though the influence of a sterner generation, the generation of Milton and Locke, was still felt, and though Newton had been their worthy successor, King George's reign was not the period, nor was the London literary circle the society, to impress a Frenchman with a just appreciation of England's moral depth or religious sincerity. Montesquieu became acquainted with England when her religious life was less active than it had been in many years. But he came at a favorable moment for observing the great change in her constitution, a change by that time already partly accomplished and partly still in operation. Many of the men with whom he associated were among the leaders of the Whig party. Constitutional liberty was their watchword. The nation had taken several great strides forward in the direction of a broader freedom, and was congratulating itself that at least no harm was done. A rationalistic party was prominent in the Church of England. Deism was fashionable in literary circles. Philosophy as opposed to theology, natural religion as opposed to revelation, seemed to be winning the day. No shock was felt at discoveries and discourses which would have brought men to the rack and stake in France. At any time, but then especially, a Frenchman bred under the old *régime* must have found England a paradise of freedom. Free speech, free printing, the right of assembly, religious toleration, taxation by Parliament only, the law of *habeas corpus*, trial by jury, freedom to move unquestioned from town to town, the suffrage, limited though it was, — all these were things unknown and almost undreamed of in France, but taken for granted, many of them as an immemorial heritage, in England. No wonder Montesquieu, and, later, Voltaire and Rousseau, were attracted to England, and received there a decided bent. Only in Britain and her colonies, and in heroic Holland, were these rights of man then maintained.

After his long and fruitful travels, Montesquieu spent two years quietly at La Brède, completing his second great work, "Considérations sur la Cause de la Grandeur et de la Décadence des Romains," which he published in 1734. It is not a large book, but covers the subject. It was impossible to treat of national aggrandizement and decline, without reference, direct or indirect, to the exalted state of France under Louis XIV., and to the symptoms of weakness which had multiplied so alarmingly under the Regent. And here we come upon the other influence which, next to the example of England, most affected French political thought throughout the first three-quarters of the eighteenth century. This was the example, apt or fanciful, of the ancient Greek and Roman commonwealths. Solon and Lycurgus, the Horatii, Cincinnatus, Brutus, and Cicero were names to conjure with. The Latin classics, particularly, were very familiar to the average educated Frenchman of that day. Those passages which celebrate liberty and the Republic were regarded with reverence, and from them French authors were accustomed to draw most of their political illustrations, so that Montesquieu's "Considérations" was in line with the taste of his age. Its originality lay in the application, more or less plainly indicated, which Montesquieu made of these old examples. The work was a specimen of real philosophy of history, useful to his contemporaries because bravely facing the issues of the time, and a permanent contribution to literature because greatly conceived and admirably written.

During fourteen years after the publication of this work, from 1734 to 1748, Montesquieu lived at La Brède and Paris, in full touch with many of the best minds of France. He was laboring on his masterpiece, "L'Esprit des Lois," a profounder work than either of the others, though perhaps not more effective than the "Lettres persanes." "L'Esprit des Lois" is one of the first and noblest contributions in modern times to the science of comparative jurisprudence. Primitive as is its method, narrow as is its statistical range, the conclusions reached are singularly numerous and sound. It is pervaded with the breath of genius. None but a deep and comprehensive mind, endowed with a veritable instinct for observing relationships, could have made so many successful generalizations on so small a basis of facts. With a rather loose arrangement, the ideas are yet very clearly presented. It is a book which contains the results of much reading and more thinking. Each page seems the product, the secretion, of a lifetime. A vast and complicated subject is reduced to a simplicity which, though perhaps illusory, is certainly fascinating.

Even in this calm, scientific work, the

outcome of an orderly and studious life, we can plainly discern the revolutionary bias. By the mere fact that he showed Frenchmen the possibility of living under law in some other than a despotic *régime*, Montesquieu awakened longings for a change. But he went further. He states that there are three forms of government, — despotic, monarchical, and republican, and defines them thus: "The republican government is that in which the people as a whole, or only a part of the people, possess the sovereign power; the monarchical, that in which only one person governs, but by fixed and established laws; whereas in the despotic government a single person, without law and without restraint, determines all things by his will and his caprice." Full of respect and admiration for the republics of antiquity and the constitutional government of England, and employing as his chief argument their success and the happiness of their subjects, he hesitates between monarchy and republic, but never falters in his impeachment of despotism, which we must remember was the French form. And the most brilliant part of the book, where his faculty of divination has freest play, is the chapter on the English

People and the chapter on the French Monarchy. He does justice to the English character and constitution, magnificent justice for a Frenchman, and such as no other of his countrymen has ever done before or since, not excepting even Taine. And, finally, I do not know any subtler characterization of the French spirit than this: Society life under the monarchy " is the school of what is called *honor*, the universal master who shall be everywhere our guide. Three things we observe there and find constantly mentioned: that our virtues should be touched with a certain nobleness, our morals with a certain freedom, our manners with a certain politeness. The virtues exhibited in this society are always less what one owes to others, than what one owes to one's self; they are not so much a response to an appeal from our fellow-citizens, as a mark of distinction between us and them. In this society men's actions are judged not as good, but as handsome; not as just, but as great; not as reasonable, but as extraordinary. When honor can point to something noble in them, it becomes the judge, and renders them legitimate, or the sophist, and justifies them."

As may be inferred even from these citations, Montesquieu was both a destructive critic and a constructive critic. He attacked abuses; but on almost every page, especially of "L'Esprit des Lois," he proposes as a substitute for despotism the institution of a limited monarchy. He acquaints us, therefore, in advance with the double aspect of the Revolution, with the revolutionary analysis and the revolutionary synthesis.

THE REVOLUTIONARY ANALYSIS

VOLTAIRE

THE REVOLUTIONARY ANALYSIS

VOLTAIRE

MONTESQUIEU'S life-work was an attack on the existing state of things in France by disclosing the political causes of oppression and by offering constitutional monarchy as a substitute for absolutism. His method was scholarly rather than popular, subtle rather than sensational, — so scholarly, so subtle, and on the whole so cautious, that he escaped persecution and his works found a welcome in unexpected quarters. They were regarded complacently by courtiers and tax-collectors, and with tolerance by bishops. Speculative essays in the sphere of politics were not yet capable of exciting passion, because the possibility of revolution was scarcely dreamed of. Besides, Montesquieu, except by innuendo in the "Lettres persanes," did not undertake systematically the more serious task of criticising the national religion and the national culture, which were even more intimate elements of national life.

Government is external and uninfluential as compared with these two factors, which constitute in largest measure the lives of individuals first and then of the community. Men who might contemplate with indifference a change in the government would resent the slightest criticism of their personal beliefs and habits. It is one thing to be told you do not live under the best possible form of government, and a far more startling thing to be told that your religion is folly, your science antiquated, and your conduct irrational. Montesquieu was not severe except in his judgment of the political system under which France groaned. Yet religion and education needed reform even more than did the government. The peasantry were little better than heathen. Their religion was little above paganism. The *bourgeoisie* were almost as bigoted as the peasants, without the saving grace of simplicity. Religion in the noble class was almost wholly formal. The peasantry were illiterate. The education of the *bourgeoisie*, the middle or trading class, was in the hands of the clergy, and managed entirely in the interest of the Church. Even the best schools, which were patronized by the aristocracy and the wealthier *bourgeoisie*, taught nothing well except languages and mathematics. Physical science, nowhere beyond its childhood at that time, was in its infancy among the French. Medicine and surgery had made little progress in France since the sixteenth century. In philosophy Descartes and Pascal had had no worthy successors, and even the speculations of these great metaphysicians were withheld from all but the most advanced students. Of course, modern history was unfairly taught.

It would seem that here was an impossible task, — to make people conscious of their condition, and then to introduce a purer religion, or a substitute for religion, and a new intellectual life. But some men are everywhere to be found, not necessarily the strongest or finest spirits, who are protestant and dissident at heart, ready for a change, ready to form a radical party. It may be easily imagined, then, that there were burning hearts in France during the reign of Louis XV., inaptly called the "Well Beloved." But free thought dared not employ free speech. It would, however, have been strange if among the enlightened few in France, heirs of the wit of Rabelais and Molière, bred on Montaigne's questioning philosophy, and encouraged by Montesquieu's success, there had not been one man bold enough to speak out against intellectual and religious oppression.

The man was already born, — Voltaire, the incarnation of the revolutionary spirit. It is convenient, perhaps even too convenient, to study the literature of the Revolution, particularly in its analytical phase, through the life and works of this great representative. If Montesquieu is the strategist, and laid down with academic coolness the lines on which the battle should be fought, Voltaire is the general, with whom we associate the strife itself. He bore the burden and heat of the day. He lived a long, conspicuous life, more than sixty years of which were years of immense productiveness and unusual publicity. His field of action was broader than Montesquieu's, for he concerned himself not so much with theories of government as with the whole world of thought, — with social studies, natural science, philosophy, morality, and religion. Indeed, considering the effects of his teaching, it is remarkable how little attention he paid to questions of government. He was in fact not ill at ease in a despotism, and certainly if he dreamed of a republic he had no thought of its being a possibility for France.

It is chiefly as a revolutionary writer that the world regards him now; but he was not merely that either, and his contemporaries valued other qualities in him more highly than they did his reformatory zeal.

Perhaps it is nearest the truth to say that, as the foremost man of letters in France, he translated and illustrated revolutionary tendencies which originated in society at large. Literature, not politics or even philosophy, was his profession. Yet by every passing generation Voltaire's literary work is less and less enjoyed, while his place as a factor in the Revolution is becoming more and more assured. His poems, his plays, his novels, which were once deemed immortally bright, have taken on somewhat of the dull hue of age. We read them now, not for themselves, but for what they reveal of their author and his century. Historical interest has superseded intrinsic interest. The reason for this is plain. Voltaire as poet and dramatist was a continuator of Boileau and Racine; he reflects the calm and steady radiance of these great masters. On the contrary, the personal, social, political, and philosophical side of his work gives light of itself, and is frankly of the eighteenth century.

And since he was the central literary figure in France throughout the second and third quarters of the eighteenth century, he is the most valuable witness to what the thought and feeling of that time really were. His own contribution to revolutionary forces was, of course, only what one man could do, and that was small in comparison with the deeper swelling of popular revolt. But it was perhaps the principal individual contribution. And coming early in the struggle, Voltaire's influence was necessarily destructive. We shall therefore be simplifying our work if we take him as the representative of the analytical forces in literature which were part of the French revolution.

His real name was François Marie Arouet. He was born in Paris, in 1694, and died there in 1778. His father was a rich lawyer, and his family on both sides belonged to the *haute bourgeoisie*, or upper middle class. He received his education from the Jesuits, at the Collège Louis-le-Grand, where he was quickly recognized by his masters as a boy who could write. They took pains to cultivate his aptitude for composition, and it is worth noticing how much attention was paid to this matter in an age when education in most other branches was superficial. The most significant feature of Voltaire's youth is that he early conceived it to be his mission in life to write poetry, and made distinct and well-regulated efforts to educate himself to this end. The influences which surrounded him were bad. His cleverness made him welcome to a group of dissipated older men, men of intellect, but without morals, several of them concealing under priests' gowns the hearts of infidels and the lives of libertines. For him henceforth it was impossible to conceive of a clergyman who could possess at the same time intellectual candor and moral uprightness. Mr. Morley remarks that probably the only sincere and decent person of the whole set was the celebrated courtesan, Ninon de l'Enclos, who died in 1705, at the age of ninety, when Voltaire was eleven years old, and left him a legacy for the purchase of books. Young Arouet's father did what he could to extricate him from bad company, by getting him an appointment under the French ambassador in Holland, whither the young man went with high hopes of seeing the world and pursuing his vocation of poet. At the Hague he fell in love with the daughter of a French lady living there in exile, and the ambassador sent him home. Up to this time he had been nothing but a wit, — a writer of minor verse, chiefly satirical. But after his return, when he was twenty-two, an epigram of his against the Prince Regent was widely circulated, and he was accused falsely of having written a number of satirical verses called *Les J'ai vu*, describing the wretched condition of France and the malignant power of the Jesuits. He was thrown into the Bastille on a *lettre de cachet*, and imprisoned there nearly a year. His incarceration ripened him, and after that he too could say *J'ai vu.*

He employed the time of his captivity in writing plays, and beginning what he determined should be the great epic of France, "La Henriade," a poem celebrating the life and times of Henri IV., the king who, more than any other since Saint Louis, had made an impression on the hearts and imaginations of the French people. For seven years after his release, in 1718, he continued working at this, and always had a play or two on hand, for he aspired, even till his death, at the age of eighty-four, to win a place with Racine as a great tragic poet. These seven years were spent going to and fro among rich, dissolute people, who entertained him at their houses, enjoying his witty conversation and aiming to be thought patrons of literature.

In consequence of a quarrel with a scion of the noble house of Rohan, who had him horsewhipped by his lackeys for an epigram, Voltaire was again imprisoned, and on his release was exiled from Paris. Providing himself with letters of introduction to certain of the celebrities of England, he fled to that land of liberty. This was in 1726. His narrative of his first impressions of the Thames and of London is one of the freshest and most delightful passages in his works. He liked the country. He liked the people. He flourished in the air of freedom. With characteristic zeal he fell to work on the English language, and mastered it, as few foreigners ever do, becoming proficient not only in composition, but in speech. His sojourn in England, from 1726 to 1729, directly preceded the visit of Montesquieu, who lived there from 1729 to 1731.

I have remarked that Voltaire conceived of himself first as a poet. He subsequently added to this conception another. He began during his English residence to regard himself as a warrior in the struggle of religious thought. Henceforth there is scarcely a line of his but was intended as a contribution to this strife. On the termination of his exile, in 1729, he returned to France with an improved edition of "La Henriade," a play entitled "Jules-César," the unfinished manuscript of his "Lettres sur les Anglais," and his "Histoire de Charles XII." The "Lettres sur les Anglais" began with an easy narrative of his arrival in London and a description of the things there which seemed most curious to a Frenchman. Their principal themes, however, are three, sometimes boldly enounced, sometimes deftly insinuated; namely, the advantage of religious toleration as practised in England, the excellence of the English in administration and commerce, and the respect paid in England to science and literature. The titles of the letters are as follows: England, The Quakers, Anglicanism, The Presbyterians, The Socinians or Arians, Parliament, The Government, Commerce, Vaccination, Lord Chancellor Bacon, Mr. Locke, Descartes and Newton, Gravitation, Mr. Newton's Optics, Infinity and Chronology, Tragedy, Comedy, Lords who cultivate Literature, Rochester and Waller, Pope and others, The Respect due to Men of Letters, The Academies, Anglomania.

"Les Lettres sur les Anglais," following on the heels of Montesquieu's "Lettres persanes," produced a sharp awakening in France. Their tendency was not so cunningly masked as that of the "Lettres persanes," and the government was by this time aroused to the danger of such comparisons. So the book, although probably completed and printed in 1731, seems not to have been really published till 1734, when five editions appeared. Voltaire's hesitation about publishing was justified by the prosecutions with which he was at once threatened. He was obliged to flee from Paris to avoid arrest.

The "Histoire de Charles XII." is regarded by many persons as Voltaire's most perfect work. It had, moreover, great contemporary interest. Charles, King of Sweden, after a short, meteoric career of military prowess, had been killed at the siege of Frederikshald, in 1718; so that Voltaire was writing very modern history in recounting his adventures. The book became at once, and has remained, a classic. It has almost the conciseness of Cæsar's Commentaries, with a fluency and rapidity peculiarly Voltaire's. It put him in the first rank of living historians. He next threw himself with passionate energy into that "Histoire du Siècle de Louis XIV.," which is now regarded generally as his greatest single work.

By this time he had published or had caused to be circulated in private, not only the serious works above mentioned, but other productions serious in a different sense,—serious in the object of their attack and in their consequences for him. These were epigrams, short poems, numberless letters, and especially the first cantos of a blasphemous satire on the sacred story of Jeanne d'Arc, that most ideal figure in French history and in the hearts of Frenchmen. This infamous jest, which he began in 1730 and strung out over a large part of his life, was entitled "La Pucelle." Its cynical baseness and profanation of religion, even more than its satirical references to the ancestors of powerful houses, completed Voltaire's disfavor with the authorities. They interfered now with all his publications, subjecting them to a galling censorship, and often forbidding him to print or sell his books. For a long time even "La Henriade" was under the ban.

Voltaire's bitterness and assiduity in attack were intensified by something which occurred in 1730. The celebrated actress, Adrienne Lecouvreur, who was a friend of his, was refused burial in consecrated ground because of her profession and because she had died without absolution. Her body was conveyed in a common cab, by a squad of policemen, to a spot outside the town. Voltaire's trend of mind was further strengthened by the "convulsionist miracles" which excited Paris in 1731. It was reported that miraculous cures were wrought at the tomb of a deacon who died in 1727. Many persons of high standing in Paris, members of the austere Jansenist party or sect, resorted to the spot, where they suffered violent convulsions and prophesied. The authorities, to put an end to the excitement, closed the cemetery in which the deacon was buried. The question of the possibility of miracles was hotly debated, and the authorities were accused of inconsistency.

In 1733, Voltaire formed a liaison with a woman celebrated at that time as a mathematician and physicist, Madame du Châtelet. Although her husband was living, and not at all on bad terms with her, she took Voltaire into her château at Cirey, near the southern border of Alsace, and lived with him sixteen years. She possessed considerable wealth, and Voltaire, too, had begun to accumulate his vast fortune. Cirey was separated from the world by many miles of abominable roads. He was safe there from all enemies except *ennui*. Madame du Châtelet was a remarkable woman, a mathematician of some note, a diligent student of philosophy, and an unwearied if not very successful writer. She kept Voltaire at her château at various times and for various lengths of time. This man of world-wide note was a slave to the caprice of an unhappy, unbalanced woman. According to their own accounts, they worked hard at their separate literary and scientific occupations, inspiring each other's zeal for knowledge and helping each other in composition. Voltaire was possessed at this time with a lively but superficial interest in mechanical and chemical experiments, and as for Madame du Châtelet, nothing seems to have been uninteresting to her. She was engaged for a long time in verifying and translating the mathematical works of Sir Isaac Newton. According to Voltaire's statements, which are not always trustworthy, they often toiled sixteen hours a day. A most uncommon love-affair this, and not very idyllic. Altercations, lawsuits, jealousies, literary quarrels, and petty annoyances of all kinds are the principal themes of his letters from Cirey.

The record of the years at Cirey, in a gloomy château, miles from any town, and several days from Paris, with a woman who swung between hard deism and silly sentimentality, is reading stupid enough to make one almost doubt if this captive Odysseus were really Voltaire, elsewhere the mortal foe of *ennui*. Poetry was getting further than ever beyond his reach, as he lost whatever of poetic calmness and poetic purity he once possessed. He lived now, his enemies declared, like a jackal of the desert, outside the haunts of men, but unable to keep from howling at them in the dark. For he kept up a vigorous warfare against the Church and State, against custom, prejudice, ignorance, and superstition. Meanwhile he was becoming enormously rich, by shrewd investments. His fortune continued to increase until, at his death, he was for those times a very great capitalist. Amid all the pettiness of this part of his life, when vanity and hate made him an unhappy and uncompanionable man, there was one plain-featured but essential virtue which he exercised to an unusual extent. I mean the virtue of industry. Never did a man live more completely for his idea. Never did a man toil more unremittingly. He knew the objects of his attack to be so numerous and thick-skulled that not merely must his sword be keen, but its blows rapid. The man who would make any lasting impression on the superstitions and prejudices that propped the standard of absolutism must not only speak bold words, but keep on speaking them.

A great deal may be said against Voltaire's mode of attack. It was often unfair. He habitually said one thing, and meant another and more offensive. He wrote many plays, for instance, particularly at this period, 1729–1750, between his return from England and his departure for Berlin, which contain hidden arguments against Christianity, or ridicule which is even more insidious. Of such may be mentioned "Zaïre," 1732, "Alzire," 1736, "Mahomet," 1741, "Mérope," 1743, and "Semiramis," 1748.

On the other hand, it is true that the vigilance of his enemies made it impossible for him to speak openly. He was a broad mark for persecution. No movement of his escaped the notice of fanatical opponents, whose methods were not more honorable than his own. It is true that he turned thousands of hearts away from Christianity by ridiculing the follies and inconsistencies of professed Christians. He led men to hate religion who had never read a reasoned argument against it. Few really strong spirits were perverted by him, for his arguments are not substantial, being based on a totally inadequate foundation of scriptural and historical scholarship. While admitting the existence of God, he denied the authority of the Bible, the possibility of miracles, the divinity of Christ. Yet for biblical criticism he was not well equipped. Nevertheless, he succeeded in creating what we might almost call a national attitude of mind toward these high questions, and to this day there exists a large class of Frenchmen in whom his moral and mental temperament still lives. A hundred years ago, to be a middle-class Frenchman was to be a Voltairian, three times out of four. It is unfortunately the case in Latin countries that when men revolt against the superstitions of the popular religion they generally fall into atheism, or an empty deism, which to all practical intents is nearly the same as atheism, and this is particularly true of the shrewd but narrow-minded French *bourgeoisie*. They are hard, unimaginative, wedded to material things, and quick to draw insufficient conclusions from a small appearance of fact.

Yet, after all, and acknowledging the harm he did to many minds of his own and later generations, we cannot altogether condemn Voltaire for his fierce and subtle attack upon what passed for Christianity in France. There was more superstition than true religion, more spiritual tyranny than meek and lowly faith, in the Roman Catholic Church of his day and country. To many of the best minds of Europe his voice was the trumpet-call of a deliverer.

Young men especially lent a ready ear. One of the strongest and most youthful spirits then in the world was the Crown Prince Frederick of Prussia, later known as Frederick the Great. Brought up under martial rules by a despotic father, this enthusiastic young man of genius had not yet tasted liberty, and he longed to expand, to put into action his palpitating emotions, to array his intellectual forces against great independent thinkers. One day in the toilsome retreat at Cirey Voltaire was surprised by a long, ardent letter from the Prussian prince. This was the beginning of a voluminous correspondence. Madame du Châtelet grew jealous. It was with difficulty Voltaire persuaded her to let him meet Frederick at the frontier of Rhenish Prussia. But in 1749 she died a most sad and tragic death, and Voltaire was free to accept the invitation of Frederick, now king of Prussia, to go to his court at Berlin and Potsdam. He was never safe from prosecution in France, and besides was of a restless disposition. His vanity, moreover, was tickled by the prospect of living as a distinguished guest at a court which, although far inferior in splendor to the court of Versailles, was already beginning to claim a rival eminence as a centre of learning. Frederick, himself an author, and a very voluminous author, of French prose and verse, was inaugurating his reign by upbuilding not only the military but the commercial and intellectual power of Prussia. His vast extension of the army came later. It is strange that his scheme for developing the resources of his country did not include strengthening the position of the German language and the production of a native literature. Since the age of the Reformation there had scarcely been a living German literature, and in polite circles the German language was regarded as the speech of boors. Though his heart was German to the core, Frederick the Great desired to be in outward things like a French monarch.

His purpose in drawing Voltaire to Berlin was to strengthen the national Academy, which he was fashioning after the model of the French Academy. It was a great stroke to capture the most notable living man of letters. Frederick and Voltaire and their Academy exerted a considerable influence on the intellectual development of Germany. They furnished the leading minds of the country with a centre of movement. They introduced somewhat of French distinctness into its hitherto vague intellectual atmosphere. They gave definiteness to public questions. Their influence on religious thought in Germany was destructive, for the time being, and had much to do with the sceptical awakening or *Aufklärung*, which, with all its obvious advantages, was not an unmixed good. An attack which in France might be authorized by the debased condition of the Church, superstition having there in large measure taken the place of true religion, would not have the same justification in Protestant Germany. The three years of Voltaire's sojourn at Berlin and Potsdam had, moreover, a baneful effect upon the development of German literature. He helped to make the German language and native German ideas unpopular with the upper classes, who were induced by his ridicule and Frederick's example to neglect and despise the riches of their own country. French became more than ever the language of the Prussian court. French plays occupied the theatres. Even private correspondence was generally conducted in French. This was the darkest period in the history of German literature. For a whole generation these conditions prevailed, until Lessing, that brave, original, and patriotic man, by the conscious devotion of a lifetime, stirred his fatherland to shame and taught her to look to herself for regeneration.

Voltaire's visit was brought to an end in 1753 by his own irascibility and Frederick's growing independence of character. The latter revolted against his guest's trickiness, yet was not above meeting it with a mixture of brutality and subterfuge. Voltaire quarrelled also with another celebrated

Frenchman, Maupertuis, upon whom Frederick counted to lend distinction to his Academy, in physical science and mathematics. The outbreaks of fury and sarcasm which accompanied these disagreements were notorious throughout Europe, and Voltaire was chiefly responsible for this publicity. There was little of philosophic decorum, or even of ordinary good manners, displayed in these singular quarrels, which were not by any means the only ones of their kind between "philosophes." Indeed French men of letters in the eighteenth century were not as a rule distinguished for nobility of conduct or refinement of spirit. In this they present a marked contrast with their predecessors of the seventeenth century. Untruthfulness, jealousy, pretentiousness, contempt for social virtues, want of appreciation for poetry, art, and religion, — these bad qualities were common to nearly all of them. On the other hand, we find a praiseworthy devotion to the cause of free thought, and unflagging industry.

After returning from Germany, Voltaire purchased an estate at Ferney, in the free republic of Geneva, just across the French line. Here he built a home and entered upon a new life, as farmer on a large scale. The Calvinists of Geneva did not seriously disturb his repose, and he was safe from arrest by the French police. It was from this retreat that he sent forth another of his greatest works, the "Essai sur les Mœurs et l'Esprit des Nations," in which, more than in any other production, he embodied his so-called "philosophical" views and his ideas upon the politics and religions of the past. It is very largely concerned with casting ridicule on the historical books of the Old Testament and in discrediting Jewish writers and the Church fathers. In the light of modern investigations, even by the most anti-Christian scholars, his arguments appear superficial and childish. In fact, he was wont to produce his effects, not by argument at all, but by mere assertion. It is astonishing that he could ever have been regarded as a serious biblical critic.

It is difficult to make a chronological survey of Voltaire's works, because he wrought at many things simultaneously, holding numerous unfinished pieces in hand for a long time, often publishing anonymously and surreptitiously, and revising thoroughly his successive editions. During his life at Ferney he was especially active. He was writing thousands of letters, both private and open; he was publishing poetry, mostly satirical, but occasionally more earnest, as his famous verses on the Lisbon earthquake, which are perhaps the only real poetry he ever made; he was turning out a play nearly every year and having them performed at his château, thereby exciting the disapprobation of his Calvinist neighbors; he was sending off articles for the Encyclopédie of D'Alembert and Diderot; he was printing essays on all sorts of subjects,—literary, legal, and theological; he wrote several novels and many short stories.

In March, 1762, there came to him at Ferney a traveller from the south of France. This person related a story which, if true, would be ample justification for the hatred Voltaire had all his life been pouring forth against the Church, and an opportunity for a fresh campaign against that spirit of bigotry which he now always termed, in accents fierce and shrill, The Infamous Thing. A young man belonging to a Protestant family named Calas, of Toulouse, joined the Catholic Church. Shortly afterwards the dead body of one of his brothers was found hanging from a rafter in his father's shop. The aged father and other members of the household were charged with having murdered him to prevent his renouncing the Protestant faith. Several Catholic societies of Toulouse were active in stirring up persecution on this charge. There was absolutely no evidence against the Calas family, and an impartial court would have had no difficulty in perceiving that it was a case of suicide. But the court of Toulouse was far from impartial, and, moreover, was pushed to extremes by a popular wave of fanaticism. A barbarous sentence was passed upon the unfortunate family. Jean Calas, the father, was put to death by torture. His property was confiscated. His wife and children and a servant, after varying terms of imprisonment, were turned out to starve.

The effect of such a story upon Voltaire can be imagined. He was stirred at once to active and practical measures. He learned that one of the Calas boys had taken refuge in Geneva. He received him into his own house, took upon himself the support of the widow and other children, dropped his farming and building and poetry, and, having ascertained the truth of the matter, gave himself up wholly to obtaining redress. Pamphlet upon pamphlet, letter upon letter, did he write in behalf of this afflicted family. In response to his appeal contributions began to arrive from all parts of Europe, and with this money and his own fortune he was enabled to enter suit before the supreme court at Paris for a reversal of the decision of the court of Toulouse. Reversal would involve the clearing of all taint from the name of the father and the restoration of their property to his heirs. The Church party made a strong fight. The government was interested in proving the integrity of its judges and the judicial system. Voltaire was shrewd enough to win the sympathy of the king's mistress and of her favorite. Pressure was brought to bear by nearly all the literary men in France and throughout Europe. The result was victory for the cause of justice. In 1765, three years after the condemnation of Jean Calas, it was revoked and his character vindicated. His family were restored to their rights. Nor was this all. The judges of the Paris court petitioned the king to reimburse the members of the Calas family for their losses and expenses, and the prayer was granted.

Few events in the eighteenth century made

a greater stir or had more influence upon the intellectual development of the world. Voltaire was the hero of the hour, and deserved the praise which was showered upon him from the uttermost parts of the earth. If he had done no other good thing in his life, his disinterested and generous conduct in this affair, and the immense energy and ability he bestowed upon it, would be enough to make him famous, and it is not merely charitable, but just, to let his magnanimity on this occasion cover a multitude of mean and petty actions. An account of the Calas affair, including some of Voltaire's pamphlets in the case, is printed among his works with the title "Essai sur la Tolérance." The Calas affair was not the only occasion on which Voltaire rescued innocent persons from the clutches of the law, but it may serve as a specimen of the others.

The closing years of Voltaire's life saw no diminution of his literary activity. As his position in the world's esteem was more secure, he was more outspoken. His contributions to literary criticism during this time were enormous. His polemical work was even more voluminous. Nor was there any falling off in vigor. The vivacity of youth, his almost preternatural cleverness, were not diminished. The record of his old age is darkened, however, by a tricky endeavor to obtain formal reconciliation with Rome. Through the basest deception and bribery he received absolution from a venal priest, and was permitted to partake of a communion at which his heart mocked. He built a church on his estate at Ferney, over whose door he had the impudence to inscribe, "Deo erexit Voltaire." Many conjectures have been made as to the cause of this behavior, so cynical, or else so inconsistent. The most probable opinion is that his chief motive was fear of being buried as an outcast, in unconsecrated ground.

Voltaire lived long enough to see much sturdy growth from the seed he had sown, though not all the fruit was ripe, some of it very bitter and some sweet. From about 1765 to 1778, the year of his death, he was an idol in the eyes of a large number of Frenchmen, and acknowledged by all parties, except the rigidly orthodox, as an ornament of the nation. In court circles particularly his ideas had found singular acceptation. Even foreign princes, even the Empress of Russia, were his admirers. All these saw in him, not merely the greatest literary celebrity of France, but a successful, a renowned, a glorious champion in the war for freedom of thought. In other words, they worshipped in Voltaire, some consciously and others unconsciously, the spirit of the Revolution. The Revolution had been making progress since 1715. The year of the Bastille was close at hand. But in 1778, at the age of eighty-four, Voltaire imprudently visited Paris, and the fierce and fickle city, which he had with good reason feared all his lifetime, now killed him with kindness. Multitudes waited there to do him honor. From the king to the market-women, all Paris was stirred with pleasure. The street before his door was filled with crowds acclaiming the defender of the innocent, the champion of liberty, the enemy of superstition, the great national man of letters. He attended the theatre to oversee the rehearsals of one of his plays, at the public performance of which a grand ovation was expected. The French Academy gave him a solemn reception. He was overwhelmed with visits from distinguished persons, among them Benjamin Franklin. At the height of his glory, worn out with fatigue and excitement, he broke down and died. It is worth remarking that, by a continuation of his own trickery, his friends managed to smuggle his body (for he had again broken with Rome) into consecrated ground at an abbey not far from Paris. In the wild days of 1791 it was brought back and interred in the Panthéon.

In what category or categories do we find this man, so active, so untiring, so manifold in his expression of himself? He touched life at a thousand points, and impressed the stamp of his personality upon the world's soft wax. And, on the other hand, he was susceptible to the world's most subtle touch, and the lines of his character were graven by the spirit of the time. If he set his seal deep on the common mind of man, the motto of the seal, you will discover, is some formula or maxim worked out unconsciously by the world at large, and merely reaching fixed expression in his vivid intelligence. He lived eighty-four years, and was, the chief part of that time, the intellectual representative of a great nation, and more than that, of a large class in all nations. His name brings instantly to mind his century. We never say "Voltaire" without thinking of the eighteenth century, which he epitomized. No Frenchman of his time had so great fame as he in foreign countries, or was so generally esteemed by his countrymen. The world was divided then, and is still divided, in its opinion of his usefulness. To some he is a demon incarnate, the arch-enemy of Christianity and of all spiritual beauty and spiritual power; to others, the apostle of Truth. But none deny his vast and varied influence. It is with him as with Napoleon. Whether we love or hate him, we cannot be indifferent. Whether we curse his destructive meddling with what we hold dear, or applaud the beneficent changes he effected in the map of human thought, we must acknowledge him a mighty force. And to force, the force of boundless ambition, endless activity, irresistible genius, we must all bow, whether willingly or not. What was this man? For what precisely does he stand? Was he a philosopher? Certainly it was as a philosopher that his followers worshipped him, as a philosopher that the next generation after his knew him. And the eighteenth century is distinguished for its philosophy. But here we must be definite. It is not French philosophy for which that age is distinguished, but German philosophy, the deep, far-reaching speculations of Kant, not the popular commonplaces of the Encyclopedists. They were mere critics, and superficial critics too, of the mediæval scholasticism by which the Roman Catholic faith was supposed to be buttressed; but they were not sound scholars in either ancient or modern metaphysics, in either Plato or Spinoza. They evolved no system; they invented no dialectic; they revealed no secret of the mind; they discovered no unknown law of the universe. To Plato, Aristotle, Descartes, Pascal, and Locke they stand related somewhat as the music critics of our newspapers and reviews stand related to Beethoven, Mozart, and Wagner. And Voltaire is no more a philosopher than the other Encyclopedists. They were called philosophers, and by some writers the assault they made on ancient beliefs is termed the philosophical movement; but these expressions are proper only if we mean that they were advocates of philosophic doubt limited by deism, a formula of life which they neither originated nor embellished.

Perhaps we should think of Voltaire chiefly as a political reformer. If so, there must be definite and systematic attempts at political leadership to which we can point, or at least some divination on his part of the dangers and opportunities ahead. But we discover no such ambition and no such prophetic gift. Himself immensely rich and steadily advancing in favor with that noble class whose scornful patronage had been at once the delight and the agony of his youth, he was never, in spite of all his difficulties with the government, in a position to appreciate the helplessness of those who were really oppressed. His aspirations were aristocratic. On the threshold of manhood he assumed the high-sounding name, *de Voltaire,* and wrote for the amusement of the grandees who condescended to know him. In middle age he was the friend and guest of a king. In old age he built himself a château and posed as a country gentleman. Political outrages were common during the reign of Louis XV., but Voltaire preferred to take the part rather of men who were persecuted in the name of religion. There are few if any passages in his works which show him to have been conscious of the incurable corruption of the government. Moreover, he was not a republican at heart or by profession. Like Montesquieu, he was disposed rather toward limited monarchy. But despotism itself suited him fairly well when he was enjoying its favors. The grievances of the poor he could regard with complacency, except when religious bigotry was concerned in their oppression. A political reformer would have been more zealous, more sad, perhaps more angry, and especially better able to discern the signs of the times. There is nothing in Voltaire's writings, so far as I know, to indicate that he even hoped for what was to happen only eleven years after his death.

So then neither as philosopher nor political reformer is Voltaire chiefly distinguished. If we could have seen him in Paris, in 1778, at the theatre, superintending the actors who were bringing out his last drama, we should have little trouble in determining what title the great man himself most craved. He then, as always, in childhood, youth, and maturer years, regarded himself primarily as a poet, as a contestant for a seat with Corneille and Racine among the creators of high tragedy. No one who has read many of his letters can fail to be convinced of this. And he very cunningly sought to elevate himself by pulling Corneille down, in a laborious commentary on that great author, in which he points out all his faults, including with them many of his good, but unconventional, expressions. The commentary on Corneille is a marvel of stupid and jealous criticism. It serves to show whither Voltaire aspired. While Europe was ringing with applause for his book on England, for his life of Charles XII., for his "Siècle de Louis XIV.," for his "Essai sur les Mœurs," it is plain that Voltaire's ambition was by no means satisfied with these plaudits, and that the praise which touched him most was praise for his verse.

And if we had asked him in 1778 what title he thought he had won besides the title of poet, and prized next to that, he would have turned to the bundles of complimentary letters that came with every post, and to the approving cries of the multitude that stood outside his door cheering the benefactor of the Calas family and of other persons whom he had saved from Jesuit persecutions, and would have replied, "Next to the name of poet, I crave most the name of liberator of the human mind."

Does he deserve either or both of these titles? Can we at last give him unqualified praise for something, having denied so many claims in his favor. Honesty demands an admission that no foreigner is altogether competent to judge of French poetry. It is best, therefore, to submit to the judgment of the most excellent French critics in this decision. And the most excellent French critics place Voltaire very high — surprisingly high, I was about to say — as a tragic poet, next indeed to Corneille and Racine. They, moreover, rank his narrative and other verse considerably higher, as compared with other French poetry, than we are accustomed to rank the works of Pope in English poetry.

But to my mind the happiest word that has been applied to Voltaire in respect to his purely literary career is the word of Matthew Arnold, who called him a great man of letters. Voltaire, the poet, — that is not enough, for he was a great historian, struck out into a new path in history, taught his successors that history should deal with peoples, not alone with kings, with the development of institutions and the birth of ideas, as well as with wars and dynasties. His "Charles XII." and his "Siècle de Louis XIV." are notable, moreover, not merely for the new methods they inculcate, but because they are themselves valuable. They are clear, interesting, educative, full of ideas, and in the main accurate. But Voltaire was a great man of letters, not merely as poet and as historian, but also as pamphleteer, as novelist, as critic, as letter-writer. Voltaire a great man of letters! Here at last we have a phrase comprehensive enough to include all his various literary achievements. And it implies, in the sense in which Arnold used it, praise of a very high order, for he was speaking of the rare men, like Cicero, who are the depositories of a whole nation's culture, and who write with supreme ease on many and great subjects. It is natural that prose should be the chief instrument of such men, for it lends itself to so many kinds of literary production. But Voltaire used both prose and verse. Goethe is the great man of letters among the Germans, and indeed a much greater man of letters than Voltaire; for Goethe, with no less range and force, possessed a tenderness, a depth, an insight which were not in Voltaire's nature. Cicero, the orator and jurist, the critic, the philosopher, the elegant correspondent, is a closer parallel to the great Frenchman. In English literature, with all our wealth of poets, essayists, and novelists, we have no one name which suggests such combinations of versatility and power as the names of Cicero, Goethe, and Voltaire suggest.

A common characteristic of these great men of letters is the infallible perfection of their style. No matter what they deal with, the touch is sure, familiar, easy. We feel that they are at home in all they attempt. They breathe freely in the atmosphere of thought. They are vividly interested in all things,— in physical science, divine speculation, human life. Art and history allure them. At one time they yield to the spell of imagination; again they are the servants of solid fact. But under whatever influence they write, their utterance is large and noble. Words are their natural acts. Their style is always perfect. It is always personal, yet always universal. A page of Cicero, of Goethe, of Voltaire, is always unmistakably Cicero's, Goethe's, or Voltaire's. They had no need to sign their letters or put their names at the head of their works. Their styles are as individual as human voices are. And they are also universal. Cicero's Latin is the type of classical Latin. It has no solecisms, no provincialisms. Goethe's German ranges all the way from the homely diction of the peasant to the refined speech of Weimar's court. The French of

Voltaire is limpid and sparkling as a mountain brook. It is a language which the Crusaders, were they alive, could understand, and which will still be fresh and modern a thousand years hence. It has no dark places. Foreigners find it the easiest French to read. As some one says, it contains no wrinkles.

And the other claim we supposed Voltaire making, a moment ago, the claim that he was a liberator of the human mind — can that be substantiated? Yes, and amply. He was, as we have seen, no iconoclast in politics, — at least not consciously. It was against religious oppression that he aimed his shafts. However, the State religion was an essential part of the government. He could not strike one without injuring the other. By imparting to the people somewhat of his sceptical temper, he more than any other man put in play the disintegrating forces which were destined to break up the old absolutism. His cleverly masked freedom of speech was a weapon which more indignant spirits snatched from his hands and used with fearful effect. But it was from superstition especially that he liberated the nation. He thought he was destroying Christianity itself. He was not a Christian.

He did not understand Christianity. He hated the false thing that passed for Christianity in France. And he lived to see it shrink before his blows. He lived indeed to see, among the educated classes, almost a *tabula rasa*, so far as religion was concerned.

But here the whirligig of time has brought in a strange revenge. The Christian religion is to-day so much more solidly rooted in society, so much more respected, because more effective, that even the terrible Voltaire is not regarded entirely as an enemy. Christians can even afford to give him some credit for the wonderful change. His criticisms forced the defenders of religion to abandon the unnecessary outworks which they had been holding at frightful cost. His criticisms did still more: they compelled Christians to take to offensive tactics and give up the old policy of fighting behind ancient ramparts of logic and metaphysics. It is by active, aggressive, Christ-like beneficence that the new positions of the Church universal have been reached. Schools, charities, home and foreign missions, and above all a consecrated clergy and a purified society — these are the response forced from the Church by the raking fire of eighteenth-century criticism. As a liberator of the human mind, therefore, Voltaire's work was very great, although the outcome would have astonished him. His mordant satire has probably ceased to have any direct influence. His arguments and sneers are like old-fashioned fire-arms in a museum. We perceive now his lack of erudition, both linguistic and historical. We also perceive now his most lamentable deficiency, namely, that he had no personal experience of what religion can do for a man. He was blind to the very truth he liberated from error. He was insensible to all that is most touching and most convincing in the life of Christ and of His Church. Yet he did more than any other man of his time to restore the Church to her true position, for he was indeed a liberator of the human mind.

VICTOR HUGO

VICTOR HUGO

THOSE who admire force and those who admire strength will never have done disputing over the value of Victor Hugo's work. To the former, more easily impressed by abundance, variety, and vigor, he is nothing short of godlike. To the latter, whom perfection allures more than power compels, and who know that restraint is an essential quality in perfect art, he is not necessarily and obviously "the greatest poet of our age." He has fared ill with some of the best French critics, and even the popular voice in France is not so loud in his favor as it was fifteen or twenty years ago. Yet for us foreigners, who are often a considerable distance behind the times in our opinions of French writers, and slow to change our minds about them, the name of Victor Hugo still stands out more prominently than any other as representing the intellectual life of France since the fall of Napoleon. Even the defects of his character are by many of us considered typically

French. We see him absurdly conceited, excessively patriotic, a too voluminous producer of very varied works; and it is not unusual to believe him all the more French for these peculiarities. This, of course, is doubly unjust, — to Hugo, because the popular idea exaggerates a few temperamental excesses into huge and ridiculous deformities; to the French, because it is implied that they are lacking in the qualities of poise and good sense.

It must be a very superficial reader to whom French literature can appear to be in the main frivolous or eccentric. Dignity is not necessarily severe. It cannot be heavy; indeed, grace is of its essence. And dignity is the note of French literature in the seventeenth century, its Augustan age. To say that seriousness is the note of the eighteenth-century literature in France may sound less axiomatic, but I think it is even more true. No men are more serious than those who believe it to be their mission to revolutionize and reform society. We may not now take Diderot and Voltaire and Rousseau as seriously as they took themselves; but that is partly because their purposes have been to a large extent achieved, and the result is an old story to us. The note of the nineteenth century in French literature is harder to catch, perhaps cannot be caught; for the voices are many, and we are too near the stage. But if anything is evident it is that this era is marked by severe and conscientious industry. Criticism has been developed into an almost perfect instrument for quick, sure testing of literary claims. A perverse book may through neglect, through its insignificance, or indeed through its very absurdity, find a large number of gentle readers in England or America. In France less favor would be shown it. The artistic sense is more widely diffused there; life centres in Paris, where values can be readily compared; and, above all, the custom of personal journalism prevails in France. A man is not going to waste his time in reading a new book if the critic most competent to judge condemns it over his own signature in the morning paper. And if a new book is so insignificant that no critic reviews it, the condemnation of silence is even more annihilating. Then, too, the competition for literary honors is intense. The rewards are greater than in any other country: a seat in the Academy; a professor's chair in the Collège de France;

an office of dignity and pecuniary value under government; the knowledge that a successful French book will sell from St. Petersburg to Madrid, and from Amsterdam to Constantinople—all over the world, in fact; for in nearly every country people read two languages—their own and French. In this competition it may not always be the best written books that come to the front; but the chance of their doing so is immensely greater than elsewhere. And another beneficial result is the careful toil bestowed upon the preparation of books, the training to which authors subject themselves, the style and finish, the lopping off of eccentricities and crudities, the infinite pains, in short, which a writer will take when he knows that his fate depends on his pleasing, first of all, a select and cultivated audience of connoisseurs. No journeyman work will do.

It was by such a tribunal that Victor Hugo was judged, long before his name was known outside of France. And yet, although the popular voice has been immensely favorable to him for two generations, this high court of criticism has not decided the case. The position of Victor Hugo is by no means definitely established, as Alfred de Musset's is established, and Balzac's. But, whatever be the verdict, Victor Hugo, because of the power and quantity of his work, and his long and conspicuous life, certainly is the most imposing figure of this century in French literature.

It is often a questionable proceeding to make one man's life and works interpret for us the doings of his contemporaries, to try to find in one term the expression for a whole series of events. It is the most convenient method, to be sure, but not always the most fruitful or trustworthy. When, therefore, I remembered that Victor Hugo entered into prominence only a little after the beginning of our century, and that although dead he yet speaks, for the definitive edition of his works is not completed, and every year adds new volumes of posthumous books to that enormous succession; when I perceived how convenient it would be to make him the central and distributive figure of this whole epoch in French literary history, — I regarded the chronological coincidence rather as a temptation than as a help, and resolved not to yield to the solicitations of a mere facile arrangement. For I had no great belief in Victor Hugo's fitness to be called the representative and interpreter of his age. I was under the influence of the prevailing Anglo-Saxon opinion of him as an egoist, whom even the impulsions of his mighty genius could not break loose from absorbed contemplation of self.

Lowell expressed this opinion when he said: "In proportion as solitude and communion with self lead the sentimentalist to exaggerate the importance of his own personality, he comes to think that the least event connected with it is of consequence to his fellow-men. If he change his shirt, he would have mankind aware of it. Victor Hugo, the greatest living representative of the class, considers it necessary to let the world know by letter from time to time his opinions on every conceivable subject about which it is not asked nor is of the least value unless we concede to him an immediate inspiration."

Let us take another of these estimates, which might well deter one from considering Hugo as capable of representing any body of men or any mass of life. I quote Mr. W. E. Henley, in "Views and Reviews," a little volume of paradoxical challenges, which he calls "appreciations:" "All his life long he was addicted to attitude; all his life long he was a *poseur* of the purest water. He seems to have considered the affectation of superiority an essential quality in art; for just as the cock in Mrs. Poyser's Apothegm believed that the sun got up to hear him crow, so to the poet of the 'Légende' and the 'Contemplations,' it must have seemed as if the human race existed but to consider the use he made of his 'oracular tongue.'"

These are but two of the many expressions of disgust anybody may encounter in reading English or American criticism of Victor Hugo. But not discouraged by such estimates, and fortifying myself rather with the thought of how the French themselves esteem him, I began to read Victor Hugo again with a view of determining whether or not he could be accepted as the unifying representative, the continuous interpreter, of French literature since the fall of Napoleon. And as a result I can say that, for me, this one man's life and works formulate nearly all the phenomena of French literary history from the battle of Waterloo down to the present day. Except comedy and the realistic novel, he has excelled in every kind of literature which the French have cultivated during this century. With these two notable exceptions, he has been a champion, a precursor, what the Germans call a *Vorfechter*, in every great literary movement.

Nothing more deplorable can be conceived than the intellectual condition of France under the First Empire. The fine ideals of the young republic were a laughing-stock, a butt of saddest ridicule. For there is nothing men hate so much as the thought of a pure ideal they have once cherished and since shrunk away from; and the remembrance of a lost opportunity to be one's true self is the bitterest of griefs; and no reproach stings deeper than this, of a former and nobler state of conscience which was not obeyed. Liberty was borne down under a weight of circumstance all the more oppressive because it was thought that the new order of things was the natural product of the Revolution; and indeed it looked so. Literature was bidden to flourish by the despot. He posed as a protector of the arts, and at his command the seventeenth century was to begin again and a new Corneille, a new Boileau, a new Molière, were to adorn his reign. But he who conquered Italy could not compel unwilling Minerva, and the victor of the Pyramids could not re-animate a dead past. The writings of the period 1800–1815, indeed the whole intellectual life of that time, its art, its music, its literature, its philosophy, are what might have been expected.

After the downfall of Napoleon, what intellectual ideals remained for France? With what equipment of thoughts and moral forces did she set out at the beginning of this new epoch? With no equipment that was at all adequate for solving the staggering problems set for her to solve. Just think of them! She had to deal with monarchy and a state church all over again. She had to decide between the spirit of the old régime and the spirit of '89. There was a contradiction in her past, and she had to turn her back on one or the other fascinating period in her history—either on Louis Quatorze and the *grand siècle* with all its glory of treasured acquirement, its shining names, its illustrious and venerable institutions, or on the less attractive men and measures and purposes of the Revolution; and these latter, though apparently less worthy of proud contemplation, impressed the conscience and the political sense as being the things fullest of life for the dawning future. The most loyal conservative must have felt an awkward consciousness that the things he hated would in the end prevail.

Such, then, was the intellectual condition of France in 1815 — uncertainty and division and dearth of ideals and purposes, in the face of a future full of perplexing problems. But she was strangely hopeful. She has never been otherwise. The French are the most elastic people in Europe, and no defeat has ever discouraged them. And she was in love with herself as much as ever, and as fully convinced of her right to the leading place among all nations. Indeed it did not occur to her that she had ever surrendered that right.

What have been the principal lines of movement in French literature since 1815? In 1815 there were three men prominent in French letters and life: Chateaubriand, Lamartine, and Lamennais. Victor Hugo was born in 1802, and by 1817 he had become a literary man, not by intention merely, but by writing. He came upon the scene, therefore, when these three men were at the height of their activity; for Chateaubriand was born in 1768, Lamartine in 1790, and Lamennais in 1782; and they, appreciating the need of leadership in France under the newly restored monarchy, had thrown themselves enthusiastically into the work of instructing the people. Let us inquire who they were and what was the nature of their activity; or, in other words, what was the first public literary atmosphere that surrounded Victor Hugo.

Chateaubriand at the age of seventeen was a captain of cavalry under Louis XVI. When the Revolution broke out he came to America on a royal commission to find the northwest passage. He brought letters of introduction to the chief personages of the new world, and was much impressed with the simple and gracious reception given him by Washington, and with his unpretentious mode of life. After the failure of his geographical researches, the young officer plunged into the forest and started alone, on foot, for the southwest, his head full of romantic ideas about the beauty of primitive civilization, or absence of civilization, put there no doubt by Jean Jacques Rousseau, of whom he was an ardent admirer and a disciple. Chateaubriand's American itinerary has never been clear. Doubts have often been expressed as to whether he really saw as much of the country as he declared he did; and it has been proved recently that, with the best means of transportation then existing, he could not possibly have visited all the places he professed to have seen on this continent. However, there is nothing for it but to follow his own highly colored narration. We are told that one evening in an Indian wigwam he discovered a torn page of an English newspaper, and read of the ravages of the Revolution and the flight and arrest of Louis XVI. His loyalty was awakened, and after months of sentimental wanderings in the forests of the Mississippi valley, he returned to France and enlisted with the Royalists. They received him with suspicion, and even after his recovery, in exile, from a severe wound received in their cause, they refused him fellowship. He lived in London and Belgium and the island of Jersey, composing his first work, an "Essai sur les Révolutions," 1797, in which his ideas, both of politics and of religion, are still in a line with those of Rousseau. Shortly after its publication some inward experience of the reality of life and its dependence upon God gave him an impulsion in a new direction, and he began his great apology for the Christian faith, entitled, "Le Génie du Christianisme," 1802, of which "Atala" and "René" are only episodes. At this time Napoleon was re-establishing order, and as he considered religion necessary to political security, and was just then courting the Pope, he showered favors upon the young author, to the latter's manifest harm, for they made him fickle and ambitious, and turned his natural sentimentality into the most pronounced egoism. His masterpiece was "Les Martyrs," a sort of Christian epic in prose which appeared in 1809; and thereafter he was regarded as the leader in a conservative reaction back to Rome and back to royalty.

Lamartine was a writer of greater significance, though in his early years he stood in a secondary place, owing to Chateaubriand's influence with the clerical and royalist party, and indeed with all those who longed for peace and a revival of religious faith in France. His early life was as interesting as Chateaubriand's, and, like his, its years of transition from boyhood to active manhood were spent in foreign lands. His poetry is characterized by a certain softness and sweetness peculiar to itself, reminding one somewhat of English Cowper. It is contemplative and religious. Lamartine succeeded in being a guide to his people in so far as he attracted them by his beautiful verse to a more serious contemplation of themselves and the world, to a renewed interest in true religion, to an appreciation of the fact that Christianity was still alive and capable of inspiring enthusiasm. The feeling had prevailed in France that vital Christianity was incompatible with the cultivation of the fine arts. Lamartine proved this to be untrue. Apart from all question of the intrinsic merit of his work, his tendency was, like that of Chateaubriand, in the direction of recognizing religion and looking back to monarchical rather than republican France for inspiration and example.

Félicité de Lamennais lived a life whose details belong as much to the history of philosophy, or to ecclesiastical history, as to that of belles-lettres. First a priest, and the most ardent Catholic in France, he afterward turned against Rome and led a movement towards religious independence. There are few more interesting figures, chiefly because great religious leaders have been so rare in modern France. At the time when Victor Hugo was beginning to write, Lamennais was ardently engaged in an effort to establish the supremacy of Rome, not only over private conscience, but over political institutions, and although from his subsequent actions he is known to the world as a liberal and a heretic, yet at that time, having published in 1817 his "Essai sur l'Indifférence en Matière de Religion," he was the most jealous conservative and the most fiery churchman in France.

Thus a superficial glance has sufficed to show that the first movement which stirred literary France after 1815 was a reaction in favor of monarchy and Rome; that its champions were Chateaubriand, Lamartine, and Lamennais; that its effort was mainly through poetry and poetical prose; that its title to honor was its high political and moral purity; that its defect was its sentimentality; that its ultimate inefficacy was due to its running counter to the tendency of the age. Into this movement Victor Hugo inevitably fell; by it he was for a long time carried; with it he at first kept step bravely.

At this point let us take a glance at Victor Hugo's early life. He was born in 1802, of respectable and educated parents. His father was an army officer of increasing distinction under the Empire; his mother a sympathizer with the exiled Bourbons. During Victor's early childhood he, with his mother and brothers, moved about through Italy, following his father's campaignings under Joseph Bonaparte; but when the boys were old enough to attend school their mother took them to Paris, while the father fought through a guerilla war against the brigands headed by Fra Diavolo. After several years of tranquillity in France, Madame Hugo and her sons were again called to follow the fortunes of the head of the family, this time in Spain. The father won a generalship in the French army in that conquered country, and became majordomo of the palace at Madrid. The boys attended school in a college for noblemen's sons, and were badly treated by the young Spaniards, who could not forget that the French lads were the children of one of their conquerors. But after a brief sojourn in Spain they returned to Paris, and there the poet-life of Victor Hugo began, and began in earnest; for during three years, at school and at home, he composed verses of all sorts, and in 1817, in competition for a prize offered by the National Academy, he wrote an ode which, although not successful in the contest, brought him into public notice.

The next year he won a prize in the Floral Games of Toulouse, with a poem which is published among his other works, and which is one of the most remarkable productions of precocious genius known to literary history. In 1821 he had his first taste of the bitterness of life, and his boyhood came to an abrupt termination, in the death of his excellent mother. On the same day he became engaged to a young girl who had for a long time been his schoolmate and almost a member of his own home-circle. Her parents allowed his suit, but postponed the marriage until he should have proved himself capable of supporting a family. He set to work with feverish ardor and undertook almost every kind of literary production — odes, plays, novels. The first of his successes under this new stimulus were two remarkable stories, "Bug Jargal" and "Han d'Islande," stories which indicate a strange and exuberant imagination, tropical in its fervor, its singularity, its fecundity.

But it was in 1826, by the publication of his "Odes et Ballades," that he laid the real corner-stone of his fame. The king, Louis XVIII., liked the poems, for a natural reason, as we shall see, and gave their author a pension of one thousand francs, which in those days, and in economical France, seemed a large sum, and the young people were permitted to marry. It will be interesting to observe what was the character of the "Odes et Ballades." They are almost all political and religious, and all thoroughly conservative; all in praise of the Bourbons, condemnatory of the Revolution; silent as to Napoleon, or nearly so, and glowing with devotion to the Roman Catholic Church. They remind us of what Wordsworth twenty-five years earlier wrote, in a precisely contrary spirit, when he was influenced by the hopes inspired by the first events of 1789, and before the subsequent outrages changed him into a stiff British church-and-state conservative. These early effusions of Hugo are noble pieces of versification, and wonderful enough as the works of a very young man; but they cannot be called poetry of a high order, nor do they even give promise of what he was to do later, except that towards the last we begin to find poems which bid us expect great things in the way of style.

Two years afterward, in 1828, appeared a second volume of poems, "Les Orientales," a collection of dream-pictures of Eastern life, in somewhat the same manner as the efforts of Thomas Moore which were popular with young ladies of the last generation, but infinitely superior to all his "Lalla Rookhs" and other impossibilities. The fact is that some of Hugo's greatest successes in passionate, highly-colored description are to be found in this collection. He was a man whose heart grew slowly, however, and we look in vain as yet for poems which could teach us much about life and how to bear it patiently or enjoy it nobly.

But we are now in the midst of the four years during which Victor Hugo was changing his attitude towards art entirely, 1826–1830. Up to this time he had not entered specially into the business of criticism, had not made theories about writing, but simply written, either celebrating his political heroes or letting his fancy wander through distant lands, which were full of glamour because distant. He had gathered about him a circle of interesting people; indeed he was already the young king of nearly all the rising literary men and women in Paris. It was natural that there should be a great deal of discussion among them about the rules and proprieties of their art; but Victor Hugo was still, in this matter as in every other, a conservative.

In 1827 he surprised this little world of

admirers with a drama, "Cromwell," in the preface to which he expounded some advanced views in regard to dramatic writing. His opinions were debated, and all Paris was divided into their supporters and opponents. In 1830 appeared "Hernani," which he succeeded in having played at the Théâtre français, in spite of the opposition of the Academy, which saw in it a menace to good literature.

There are few exciting events in the history of literature. It is in the main a record of quiet, intellectual lives, a story of thoughts and tendencies. The account of a single border feud will present a greater number of striking incidents than the history of the forces which have produced our English poetry or Germany's philosophy. And the few memorable anecdotes of a concrete character which are scattered here and there in the chronicles of literature usually attract more attention than they deserve. Out of ten persons who will tell you that Demosthenes practised oratory by the sea-shore, with a pebble in his mouth, not more than one has any notion what his orations themselves were about. The man who is most set agog by the story of Shakespeare's poaching exploit is the least likely to have read his plays. The same thing might be said of the hubbub occasioned by the first representation of Victor Hugo's "Hernani," on February 25, 1830. There is a temptation to make "Hernani" the text of disquisitions on Romanticism, forgetting that it is a drama of high intrinsic merit, and that the question of positive value is, after all, the essential one.

Word was passed about among those who regarded Hugo's new theories with aversion, and a large and mainly hostile audience was assembled on that memorable night, the most eventful *première* since the first representation of Corneille's "Cid," nearly two hundred years before. Everybody knows what happened. Everybody knows how fashion and aristocracy and journalism combined to kill the new piece, which was said to have been written in defiance of the rules followed by Racine and Voltaire; how the regular theatre-goers hissed, and were howled at in turn by the worshippers of novelty, frowsy, long-haired young artists and penny-a-liners and students, from the left bank of the Seine, who had been brought over to support the play. One of the most sacred institutions of the French theatre is the *claque*, or body of hired applauders. Now on this occasion there was no *claque*, for the friends of Victor Hugo had distributed free tickets in the Latin Quarter, and their recipients were present, ready to raise the roof if necessary. The hissing and hooting began almost with the first line, and continued for several hours, until the actors had mouthed through the whole tragedy; and yet it was considered that "Hernani" had won the day.

To us such a way of supporting the fine arts and defending the canons of literary taste, indeed even such widespread and frenzied interest in anything except business, sport, politics, and religion, seems, to say the least, remarkable. But we must remember that the French go to the theatre even more than we go to church; that in February, 1830, it was not safe to get excited about politics in Paris; that athletics were neglected in France previous to 1871; and that possibly the French might disagree with us in our estimate of business as the chief end of man. But although we must admire the French for this fine capability of theirs, — this capability of taking an excited interest in the things of the mind, it may seem that the critics and historians have made too much of that fracas on the 25th of February,

1830, in the Théâtre français. They tell us that this was the first great fight between the Romanticists and the Classicists.

We can learn what these words mean only by getting the critics to indicate to us a piece of art-work constructed according to the Romanticists and another constructed according to the Classicists, and then comparing them and picking out the essential differences. They say "Hernani" is a drama of the Romanticists, and that seventeenth-century tragedy was classical. We find, indeed, that Victor Hugo's drama differs from Racine's; "Hernani" is based upon life in Spain, and not in Greece or Rome, and the period is the sixteenth century, and not the age of Pericles or Tiberius Cæsar. But if this is all, then Corneille was a Romanticist, for his first successful tragedy, the "Cid," is also a drama of Spanish life, and is set no further back than the Middle Ages. But, they say, this is not all: "Hernani" is romantic because it contains a mingling of the comic and the heroic, inasmuch as there are in it words and notions of common use, where the author might have employed expressions and ideas consecrated and set apart wholly to the service of poetry.

And this is true. Victor Hugo does use both phrases and thoughts that no writer of French tragedy had dared to use before. And here, rather than anywhere else, do we find what we mean when we say he was a Romanticist. The terms as applied to French literature used to be defined by saying that the essence of Classicism was the seeking of material in the life of Greece and Rome, and that the essence of Romanticism was the seeking of material in the life of the Middle Ages. A broader definition, however, is this, if any be possible: Classicism in literature consists in limiting the choice of a writer within a certain range of special terms and special ideas, these terms and these ideas being such as the best authors of the past have considered beautiful and appropriate. Romanticism is the theory — a more generous one — which would permit and encourage a writer to look for his material and his terms among thoughts and expressions more common in everyday experience, with large freedom of choice. In short, Romanticism is the recognition of the rights of modernity in art.

The theory of Classicism originated largely in Racine. At any rate it is purely French in origin. The old stupid German Classicism which Lessing demolished, the eighteenth-century English Classicism which Scott and Wordsworth demolished, both had their source in France. And in France Racine ruled supreme. He built his tragedies after a severe pattern, and made them very beautiful, but wholly artificial. People liked them, in that stiff and conventional age, and were far enough from investigating whether they and the dramas of Sophocles were in truth built on the same plan. They took that for granted. Henceforth to their minds there was only one way of making a tragedy: it must not violate the three unities, of time, place, and action; it must deal exclusively with exalted, heroic, and terrible emotions; it must contain only poetical expressions; it must be composed in Alexandrine couplets, with certain minor points of agreement with the versification of Racine. In short, a writer of tragedy must think like Racine and rhyme like Racine, and, above all, he must never under any circumstances employ a term or indicate an action which might be called vulgar. From France the fashion spread all over Europe. It affected Italy, even down to Alfieri, who at the end of the last century was hampered by this spirit of obedience to Racine. It made English literature of the eighteenth century what it was, and kept it from being what it might have been. Her acceptance of this theory was one of the reasons why Germany had no literature of great account from the time of Luther and Hans Sachs to the day of brave old Lessing, who was the first man of consequence to see what was the trouble, and to set to work remedying it by destructive criticism and constructive example. If it is one of the glories of Germany that Lessing was the sharpest-eyed man in Europe and the first person sound enough, independent enough, blunt enough, and skilful enough to change the fashion; to us of English speech belongs the pride of saying that it was back to Shakespeare's large humanity that the reformers turned.

We have seen that the conservative reaction, represented by Chateaubriand, Lamartine, Lamennais, and Hugo, lasted from 1815 to about 1830, and that the new spirit of Romanticism, which had been working all along, finally became dominant then. In 1828 Sainte-Beuve published his "Tableau historique et critique de la poésie française et du théâtre français," for the spirit and purpose of which, not he alone was responsible, but other young writers also. It breathed a spirit of revolt against the sterile rules which for two hundred years had stifled lyric poetry in France, and its purpose was to revive interest in the pre-classical poetry of the sixteenth century, the poetry of Du Bellay and Ronsard. Victor Hugo, wavering between his old and his new positions, was a strong influence in the life of Sainte-Beuve at this time. Literary innovations were numerous in the next two years. As usual in France, the political situation was closely connected with art-life. The political revolution of 1830, often called the Revolution of July, dethroned Charles X., and brought in, with a more liberal constitution, Louis Philippe, a prince of the house of Orléans. This event proved to be a great stimulus to literary activity and a guarantee of literary freedom. It went far towards destroying the expectation of reviving a state of society and a tone of thought modelled after seventeenth-century life. It weakened the monarchical tendency altogether, for it divided the hopes of conservatives and proved that the Bourbons were not the only possible kings of France, but that many monarchists would take a king wherever they wanted to. As is usual, and not in politics merely, but in all combinations of human effort where supremacy must be maintained by compromise, the unsuccessful minority, the hungry opposition, was freer from division, more single in aim, and purer in method, than the party in power. There is sometimes no party tonic like defeat, and nothing is so recuperative as retirement for a season. By 1830 the republican party had been so far purified by inactivity that a young poet like Hugo might be attracted towards it as to the saving remnant of his people. His drift in the direction of republicanism was hastened by the fact that his next two dramas, "Marion De Lorme," 1831, and "Le Roi s'amuse," 1832, were kept from being performed by ministerial order, because they displayed two revered kings of France, Louis XIII. and Francis I., as shallow, pleasure-loving men.

A new era for French literature began in 1830. We are justified in saying this, because the great names of the former decade had lost their brilliancy, and another set of writers had begun to be celebrated and to be looked upon as establishing the tone of thought. The character of the product, too, is different. There was a larger freedom in the choice and treatment of subjects; the literatures of England and Germany were being studied and translated. For the first time, also, was there in France any considerable appreciation of Dante.

As Chateaubriand, Lamartine, and Lamennais set the tone in 1815, so Hugo with his friends and others of the same free spirit did in 1830. About this powerful, enthusiastic man and his cultivated young wife, in their simple home, there gathered a number of literary men and women, who were called the *cénacle* or symposium. They, with other persons whom their influence touched, had a common tendency, which in the case of some was clearly enough defined to be called a common conscious purpose.

They hoped, these brilliant enthusiasts, to bring about a new French Revolution, bloodless, of the spirit rather than of the form. Here are their names: Lamartine (for he had gone over to the Romanticists), Victor Hugo, Alfred de Musset, Béranger, Alfred de Vigny, Balzac, George Sand, Alexandre Dumas, Sainte-Beuve. Although the original revolt was against the dramatic fetters imposed by

Racine and Boileau and Voltaire, the revolution had extended over the whole range of literature — against conventionality in criticism, in lyric poetry, in fiction; just as the revolt of the American colonies soon got far beyond the original grievance about the stamp tax. Their common tendency was protest against conventionality. They went too far under this impulse. Victor Hugo, the devout, God-fearing youth, became, for the time being, a sentimentalist and skeptic; a poet could not do worse, and the effect is seen in a marked diminution of creative force. He no longer possessed his old earnestness, and thus his work of this period fails to touch our hearts with fire. The self-consciousness of youth, instead of melting into that ever-present recognition of the Divine which is the true culture of a mature man, only stiffened into an odious self-conceit, which is Victor Hugo's ugliest blemish. George Sand advocated and practised free-love. Béranger, the Robert Burns of France (but not nearly so great a poet), overdid his office of convivial songster. Dumas' private life was a long scandal. His lack of restraint affected his work, for had he possessed more restraint he would have written fewer books, and they might all have been as good as "Les Trois Mousquetaires."

Alfred de Vigny is a beautiful exception. Although he followed Victor Hugo with all the ardor of his chivalrous nature, he preserved at the same time a measure, a moderation, a grace, a consistency, which the coldest Classicist might have envied. He was born in 1799, of a family of soldiers, and tells us he learned war at the wounded knees of his warrior father. In his early life he was constantly laying down the pen for the sword. While in garrison at Paris he was to be found chiefly in the libraries, and it was in camp, in the Pyrenees, that he wrote his celebrated historical novel, "Cinq Mars." His translation of "Othello" was badly received in 1829. He cultivated English literature assiduously, and drew inspiration from Milton — and Ossian. The rhapsodies of the pseudo-Ossian were causing a great stir throughout Europe, and were eagerly read and applied by the Romanticists as a proof of what could be done in defiance of the rules of Boileau. Alfred de Vigny, too, like almost every novelist from that day to this, was profoundly influenced by Walter Scott. He wrote several original plays, of which the best known is "Chatterton." But the works from his hand which our generation reads most are "Cinq Mars" and his lyric poems.

Alfred de Musset was a poet of such great importance that it is impossible to say, in a brief sketch like this, anything at all adequate about his delicate qualities of heart and mind, his strange, sad life, his wonderful achievements, and his growing fame. He will live perhaps when all his contemporaries are forgotten, except Hugo.

Balzac, George Sand, and Dumas it is hardly necessary to mention in this connection: they have the advantage of being read more than the poets. The development of the novel has been the only concerted movement of great importance in French literature since the early days of Romanticism. From Balzac, the father of the realists, Hugo, the extreme of idealists, learned little. There seems to be absolutely no artistic relation between them. George Sand and Dumas were, of course, idealists, romantic to the last degree, and although Hugo in his novels manifestly strains after reality, he is much more in line with them than with Balzac. But Hugo is not a novelist at all in the sense that Balzac or George Sand or Dumas are novelists. He has written great prose works of imagination, "Les Misérables," "Les Travailleurs de la Mer," "Notre Dame de Paris," "Quatre-vingt-treize," but the matter in each case is essentially poetical.

Sainte-Beuve passes this severe condemnation upon all the poetry of himself and his friends, at this epoch, saying: "The result of this concourse of talent for several years was a very rich body of lyric poetry, richer than France had dreamed of till then, but very unequal and diversified. Most of the poets gave themselves up, without restraint, to the unbridled instincts of their natures, and also to all the pretensions of their pride, and even to the biddings of their silly vanity. Good and bad qualities sprang up indiscriminately, and posterity will have to choose between the two. No product of the poets of that day will endure in a complete form."

But Victor Hugo outlived all parties and groups and associations of which he was a member in that early time, and his life subsequent to the exciting days of 1830 was a steady development, and contains in itself a reflection of nearly everything that was going on in France.

We may consider him under three aspects:

as dramatist, novelist, and lyric poet. He is greatest under the last aspect. Through all his life he expressed himself in song. Perhaps no other poet has done this so thoroughly, so beautifully, and for so long a period. So we may reserve the subject of his personality and actual experiences until we come to consider his lyric poetry, and glance first at his work for the stage and in prose fiction.

In 1827 appeared a so-called historical drama, "Cromwell," which was not remarkable for much except its lack of historical truth, and its preface, in which the young man outlined his theories and laid down the programme of attack upon the classical ideas. This attack was in reality first made in force with "Hernani" in 1830. "Marion De Lorme," which appeared in 1831, is a much weaker play, and abounds in the excesses to which Romanticism was prone. Apart from the substance, which is repulsive and harrowing, when not trivial, the form of the drama is loose, and one can very easily understand how such a production would offend an ear trained to the stately, chaste, and elegant dialogue of the elder poets. If this is all Romanticism has to offer, let us have back our Corneille and Racine. "Le Roi s'amuse" (1832) suffers from the same faults, and offends even more against good taste. These pieces are both strong in the main, though there are weak passages in both, but their strength is not healthy or beautiful. Victor Hugo himself called attention to the fact that he depended for his effect, in these two plays, upon the principle of contrast. It is a principle which he has employed in nearly all his work too deliberately and too exclusively. In "Le Roi s'amuse," for example, he has chosen a most repulsive figure, Triboulet, whom he makes hideous both externally and internally, by every device known to art, and in this character he implants a pure flower of paternal love. Then he stands off and says: "Behold what have I done! How deformity looks black behind that white virtue!" The principle is useful, but he makes a forced application of it. In his novels, too, every reader will recall instances where a contrast has been insisted upon till one's patience is exhausted.

"Lucrèce Borgia" (1833) illustrates the same point. It is a piling of horror upon horror for the sake, apparently, of bringing into sufficient relief a few passages of great moral beauty. This is as undignified as it is useless. Virtue needs no such setting. Vinet says that in this drama Hugo pandered to the false taste of the age, which demanded horrors and violence and sensuous appeals, instead of leading it, as he could, to follow better principles of taste.

"Marie Tudor" (1833) is, like "Cromwell," unhistorical. It is not one of Hugo's greatest plays, nor is "Angelo" (1835), another drama, in prose, and founded on history; but "Ruy Blas" (1838) is generally acknowledged to be, after "Hernani," the best of his dramas. It was followed, in 1843, by "Les Burgraves," the last of his plays written for the stage.

We have seen that at a very early age Victor Hugo wrote two stories, "Bug Jargal" and "Han d'Islande." In 1831, while in the full heat of his dramatic activity, he yet found time, by shutting himself up, and going out but once for six months, to write "Notre Dame de Paris," which is one of his masterpieces of prose, an historical novel built on a scale of gigantic proportions, and presupposing exhaustive archæological research. It is a vast picture, full of glaring lights and deep shadows, of Paris in the

Middle Ages, with the cathedral of Notre Dame as background, and indeed as one of the characters.

A man who had produced so many strong plays and this remarkable novel, not to mention his lyric poetry, could not longer be refused admission into the national galaxy of great men, and in 1841 Hugo was elected a member of the Academy. Two years later he was created a peer of France. In spite of these anchors to conservatism, as one would suppose them, a title of rank and a seat among the Immortals, Hugo became more and more radical in politics, drifting gradually towards the conception of an ideal republic, and bending his course thitherward. When Louis Bonaparte, not content with his election to the presidency in 1848, overthrew the government, and proclaimed himself Napoleon III., Emperor of the French, by the *coup d'état* of December, 1851, there was no enemy more irreconcilable than Victor Hugo. The brave poet was banished, and did not touch the soil of France again till 1870, after Sedan, when the Empire had ignominiously dissolved. Although included in an amnesty, he had not been willing to return until the Babylonian woe was past. Most of his exile he spent on the island of Jersey, under the English flag. From there he issued a political pamphlet, "Napoléon le Petit," and a succession of volumes of poetry. His second great work of fiction, "Les Misérables," appeared in 1862, followed by "Les Travailleurs de la Mer," in 1866, and by "Quatre-vingt-treize," in 1874. "L'Homme qui Rit," 1866, was an unsuccessful attempt at a historical novel, with the scene in England. Of his novels "Les Misérables" is incomparably the best. "Les Travailleurs de la Mer," while powerful in its unity and intensity, is too full of technical terms and of idiosyncrasies to be either easy or pleasant reading. "Notre Dame de Paris" and "Quatre-vingt-treize" are the most popular, next to "Les Misérables."

But it is as a lyric poet, I fancy, far more than as a dramatist, a novelist, or a political pamphleteer, that Victor Hugo will be known,

> "When time has swept both friends and foes."

Unfortunately, foreign students of French literature are less likely to seek acquaintance with his poems than with his plays and novels. The peculiar character of French versification repels us. We, accustomed to a more heavily accented line, cannot quickly sharpen our ears to the delicate modulations we encounter there. But when once the ear is attuned to these fainter harmonies, a wonderful revelation is made to us in the long succession of songs that fell from the lips of Victor Hugo.

His poetry is intimately the product of his life, especially the emotions and incidents connected with his home and family. His marriage relation was one of perfect harmony, if one may judge of such matters; and he was happy in his home. His wife was evidently the companion of his thought. His children were two sons and a daughter. In this daughter the poet's deepest love was centred, and her graces are the theme of many of his loveliest songs, while her premature death by drowning, with her young husband, in 1843, was the occasion for that one of his lyrics which contains the fullest portion of moral grandeur, "À Villequier." It is the heartbroken cry of a strong man whom the hand of God has at last led back to faith and submission along paths of darkest sorrow. For it must be remarked that Victor Hugo, intoxicated with success and the atmosphere of protest which he himself had done so much to create, had for many years apparently lost sight of his young manhood's conviction of the immanence of a God in the lives of men. After his daughter's death it was in his granddaughter Jeanne that his affection took root — the same Jeanne whom he afterwards celebrated, throughout his old age, in the poems which are found in the volume entitled "L'Art d'être grand-père."

In the volumes of lyrics from 1822 to 1840, including "Odes et Ballades," "Les Orientales," "Les Feuilles d'Automne," "Les Chants du Crépuscule," "Les Voix intérieures," and "Les Rayons et les Ombres," there is a marked change in the views of the author as to religion and politics, from conservatism to radicalism, from conviction to uncertainty and almost indifference; and there seems to be a loss of energy when we compare the first with the last productions, though there is a gain, of course, in technical skill. But in all that time there was only an evolution, not a deep moral change imposed from without, for the life of his heart was, all those years, serene. His fiery indignation against Louis Napoleon poured itself out in "Les Châtiments," published in 1853, and then followed, in 1856, "Les Contemplations," which contains the ripest fruits of his genius at its prime. Here the offended patriot is for the time in the background, and although much of the thought is deeply philosophical, this collection is rich not so much in speculative poetry, as in poetry of the heart and of daily life. Domestic affection, ecstasies of joy in love, in home scenes, in natural beauty, outpourings of gratitude, solemn hymns of duty, awful agonies of grief, make this the best biography of Hugo, and one of the most touching memorials of human life.

French literature has no sweeter, deeper, more beautiful volume of poetry to show. The incomparable succession of poems in which he sings of his lost child, beginning with her infant loveliness and ending with the songs which memory dictated to him on the anniversaries of her death, are an incomparable expression of fatherly love and poignant sorrow. In "Les Contemplations" the great master lets his large and wholesome nature speak its natural language. Here is no posing, no affectation of omniscience, no striving after imperfectly conceived ideals.

Vanished is the man of public affairs, vanished the would-be demigod; and the voice we hear is bravely human, though more eloquent than the voices of other men. Pure joys, consecrated sorrows, a ripening mind, and length of days were giving to the poet faith, humility, and insight.

But his exile broke this succession of tranquil years and growing thoughts, and from 1852 to 1870, from "Les Châtiments" to "L'Année terrible," there runs through his volumes a deep undertone of solicitude for the welfare of France, and more especially of sad personal yearning to be again upon her soil. "L'Année terrible," the year of the invasion of France, the siege of Paris, and the Commune, brought him back. The very day that Napoléon le Petit followed his conquerors out of French territory, Victor Hugo entered, and, proceeding to Paris, threw himself passionately into the national defence. It may seem a strange thing to say, but this year of disaster must have been a grand and almost a joyous one in Hugo's life. It was the vindication of his exile, in so far as that had been voluntary. It gave him a chance, which he embraced, of translating his heroic words into deeds.

The rest of his life, from 1872 to 1885, was spent in conspicuous eminence, on a throne of popularity where he sat the autocrat of republican France, without a rival, and with scarce an enemy. It is true that his career as an active politician was a failure, but then it must have been soon apparent to him that he ought never to have entered upon it, and that he could be more useful and incomparably more distinguished in his own work. His lyrical history of the world, "La Légende des Siècles," of which the first part appeared in 1859, was continued in 1876 and 1883. Another volume of lyrics, "Les Chansons des rues et des bois," was published in 1865. "L'Art d'être grand-père" was published in 1876, and "Les quatre vents de l'Esprit" in 1881.

These volumes are a vast storehouse of experiments in many kinds of verse and in the expression of many kinds of thought and feeling. They impress one rather with the poet's power and resourcefulness than with artistic perfection as in "Les Contemplations." But in all he shows himself a very great and beautiful poet. He died in Paris, on the 22d of May, 1885. His funeral was a demonstration which has seldom been equalled in the world's history for solemn pomp and the proud grief of a nation.

The question of the man's personality need not enter into our estimate of a dramatist, a novelist, or a historian, though as a matter of fact it generally does. But we can hardly consider lyric poetry merely with reference to its intrinsic quality. Lyric poetry is generally a record of intimate emotions, the sublimation of a life; and this is peculiarly true in the case of Victor Hugo. For, after all, his chief subject was himself. It is certainly permissible, and we can readily understand that it is indeed almost necessary, that a lyric poet should view the world subjectively. But it is a marked characteristic of Hugo's work that he cannot get outside of himself, that he is rarely carried away by his passion for the beautiful and the true, though this passion he did really possess. So although we cannot blame his egoism as a fault, we must deplore it as a defect; for on account of it alone he falls short, in the opinion of many critics, of being a great world-poet, one of the supreme consolers and sustainers of humanity.

There is a fine essay on Victor Hugo by Mr. Frederic W. H. Myers, which all students of the poet ought to read, not only because it is a very thorough criticism of Hugo as a lyric poet, but also because it is a masterly piece of work altogether, and full of suggestions. Mr. Myers says: "In his moral nature we shall find much that is strong, elevated, and tender; a true passion for France, a true sympathy for the poor and the oppressed, a true fondness for children. Further than this it will be hard to go; so plain will it be that the egoism which penetrates M. Hugo's character is a bar to all higher sublimity, and has exercised a disastrous effect on his intellectual as well as on his moral character."

Mr. Myers seems too sparing of his praise for what Hugo did that is excellent in poetry, passing without mention some of his sweetest songs and most stirring outbursts of grandeur. His essay came as an antidote to the immoderate eulogy published just before by Mr. Swinburne, and certainly gives us a calmer estimate of Hugo. Mr. Myers, however, does not do justice to the contents of Hugo's poetry, and he was perhaps not as susceptible of being ravished by the form as Swinburne was. Yet there is truth in what Mr. Myers says when he tells us that he thinks Hugo's " central distinction lies in his unique power over the French language, greatly resembling Mr. Swinburne's power over the English language, and manifesting itself chiefly in beauty and inventiveness of poetical form and melody." Mr. Dowden speaks with high praise of Hugo's successful efforts " to reform the rhythm of French verse, to enrich its rhymes, to give mobility to the cæsura, to carry the sense beyond the couplet, to substitute definite and picturesque words in place of the *fadeurs* of classical mythology and vague poetical periphrasis." And this is indeed the chief general distinction of the Romanticists, for their searching of foreign literature and mediæval history brought them less poetical material than variety and vigor of poetical form.

Well-grounded and natural as may be the misgivings of English and American readers who have attempted an estimate of the great Frenchman, it is doubtful if he has received sufficient praise at their hands for the qualities in which he so unquestionably excels, — the immense variety of his themes, the audacity of his flights, the purity of his ideals, the sincerity of his beliefs, the subtle and yet powerful beauty of his music. Perhaps we shall appreciate better how great a poet he is if we stop to consider that, after all, he is only a poet, and not really a novelist, in any strict sense of the word, nor a critic, nor a philosopher, nor even a dramatist. For all his work is lyrical. It is all passionate, subjective, musical. "Les Misérables," "Les Travailleurs de la Mer," and the other so-called novels, are vast poems, just as Carlyle's "French Revolution" is a poem. "Hernani" is far from perfect as an acting drama. Regarded merely as a play to be read, it is full of exasperating peculiarities. It is really a succession of intensely passionate lyric lines, passages, and scenes, in which we never for more than a moment at a time are left without a sense of the author's presence. He does not let his characters work out their own fate, in any of his tragedies. He imposes his own sympathies and prejudices upon us. His opinions, his experiences, his emotions, his ideals are kept alive in our consciousness by every page Victor Hugo wrote.

I have purposely quoted some of the severest things I could find in English criticism, because I wish to conclude with words of homage, which will carry more weight if it is perceived that they were not blindly penned. It is in itself a great achievement to have done so much honest work of a high character as Hugo did. It is no small distinction to have guided a people's hopes for eighteen years from his island of exile. It is a noble end of a zealous life to have worn for fifteen years the crown of such a nation's kingship. But when even these proud honors are forgotten, children's voices will still repeat and men's hearts still echo a hundred songs of the greatest lyric poet of France.

SAINTE-BEUVE

SAINTE-BEUVE

LIKE many other French writers of exquisite prose, Sainte-Beuve's fondest ambition was to be a poet. Three volumes of passable verse bear witness to this desire. "Les Poésies de Joseph Delorme" appeared in 1829, "Les Consolations" in 1830, "Les Pensées d'août" in 1837. Although they do not lift us into a very high region of imagination, they put us on vantage-ground whence we can look backward and forward in Sainte-Beuve's life, discovering his native temper, the peculiarities of his education, and the object of his youthful enthusiasms, and fixing the point of departure for his maturer progress. They betray an inferior poet, but announce a curious discerner of literary qualities. For the single remarkable thing about them is that they contain almost the only French poetry which is due directly to the influence of the English Lake School. We can readily understand that Walter Scott and Byron, each for different reasons, should affect continental literature. We feel the power of the one or the other in Manzoni and Leopardi, in Goethe and Heine, in Hugo, Vigny, Musset. But it is with a start of surprise and pleasure, followed perhaps by an incredulous shaking of the head, that we recognize in a French dress the spirit of Wordsworth. The poets of common life — and in this lies part of their charm — are subject to a certain degree of local limitation. They are inspired by those familiar things, the details of landscape, custom, and modes of thought, which contribute largely to determine the difference between one country and another. And the Lake poets are so thoroughly English, so essentially Protestant, and have in them so little of merely specious beauty which appeals immediately to the senses, that the Latin mind does not readily domesticate itself among them on their bleak northern hills. For you must make your home with Wordsworth if you wish to know his heart. He will not cross the seas to you. Yet Sainte-Beuve, from this humble eminence of his youthful verse, greets the Lake poets not unfittingly, on the whole, as one who has returned from a delightful sojourn with them; and there is one sonnet of Wordsworth's, to mention nothing more, which he has translated in a manner approximating perfection.

The capacity to become thus sympathetically acquainted with a foreign literature would show, even in the absence of all other proof, that Sainte-Beuve, at the time these poems were written, was a Romanticist, that he was, like Hugo and Vigny, looking abroad for themes untried in France and a fresh method. But to feel the breath of the English lakes he must have gone farther afield than any other Romanticist had done. His appreciation of the most national and intimate development of English poetry prepares us to hear that there was an English strain in his blood. His mother was the daughter of an Englishwoman. His father, a revenue officer of Boulogne-sur-mer, was a man of liberal culture, and Charles-Augustin, the son, attributed to him his own taste for reading. But the influence was wholly hereditary, for the boy was born December 23, 1804, several months after his father's death. In 1818 his mother removed with him to Paris, to give him better opportunities for education, and after finishing his college studies he entered the École de Médecine. His course here was interrupted and presently terminated by an excursion into journalism. One of his old teachers, Dubois, editor of the "Globe" newspaper, encouraged him, in 1824 and 1825, to write a few book-reviews, and the new work soon absorbed his attention.

On the 2d and 9th of January, 1827, Sainte-Beuve published a review of Victor Hugo's "Odes et Ballades." His criticism, which was discriminating and yet enthusiastically favorable, resulted in his becoming acquainted with Hugo, who lived but two doors from his lodgings. At Hugo's house he was introduced to the *cénacle* or symposium of the Romanticists. He cast his fortunes in with theirs in the combat for freedom of form and a wider field of literary effort, publishing the following year a "Tableau historique et critique de la poésie française et du théâtre français au XVIme siècle," in which he aimed to give historical support to his new friends by calling attention to the spontaneous spirit and the technical variety of Ronsard, Du Bellay, and other poets of the Renaissance. These fine old writers had been contemptuously thrown into the lumber-room of barbarous antiquities by Boileau, Voltaire, and La Harpe.

Between 1825 and 1830 the Romanticists, whatever they became afterwards, were advocates of monarchy and Catholicism. In his review of the "Odes et Ballades" Sainte-Beuve had shown that he was not yet of the new school by describing their religion as "mysticism" and including the word Christianity under the category of "mythology." But by 1829 he had accomplished one of those right-about-face movements for which he was to become notorious, and his poetry shows him, like the Hugo of that time, standing near the steps of a throne which, for all its pomp of outward decoration, has a sinister resemblance to the guillotine. His face is towards Rome and he seems oblivious of the fact that the Revolution has much of its work still to do.

After the uprising of 1830 Sainte-Beuve again began writing for the "Globe," although it was now edited in the interests of the Saint-Simonian socialists. He subsequently disclaimed all sympathy with their religious opinions. In 1829 he had contributed to the "Revue de Paris," and he was one of the founders of the "Revue des Deux

Mondes," in 1831, and continued for many years one of its most frequent writers. Under the new political influences he wrote, in 1831, for Armand Carrel's liberal paper, the "National." Sainte-Beuve's enemies, of whom there were always not a few, have dealt very severely with him on the ground of his being a turn-coat in politics and religion. A flexible, easily-influenced mind he certainly had; he seems at times a pure intelligence, the uncolored and uncoloring medium of other men's thoughts, only his taste for style remaining his own. To an English or American observer there is not necessarily any culpable inconsistency in writing literary articles for a newspaper with the politics of which one does not agree. In France, however, the matter is not so simple, no doubt because of the complication of politics with religion and with social standing.

His nearest approach to Christian belief was perhaps in 1832, when he was under the influence of Lamennais; and traces, shallow and wavering to be sure, of this approach are to be distinguished in the novel, "Volupté," which Sainte-Beuve published in 1834. Three years later he began a course of lectures at the Academy of Lausanne, which he published subsequently as the early portion of his "Histoire de Port-Royal." This great work was not completed, however, until 1859, although the first of its five large volumes appeared in 1840. It is a monument of industry, and reveals the fact that Sainte-Beuve, even before his prime, was perfectly at home in the personal and literary history of the seventeenth century. But it lacks flow. It is too manifestly a mechanical construction. It makes quite evident that Sainte-Beuve was not at his best unless writing short articles for newspapers and reviews. However deeply impressed he may have been with the unity, the almost personal individuality, of his subject, he was not able to give these qualities to his book, which is inorganic. It purports to be not only a history of the great Jansenist monastery and its men and women, its schools and books, but also of all the people who in any way affected it or came within its sphere of influence. The author succeeds better in the unhampered flights which this last purpose allowed, than he does in giving us a systematic account of Port-Royal. The best biographies, the best histories, have always been written by enthusiasts. Sainte-Beuve had only an impersonal, and towards the last an artificial interest in his grand theme. During the twenty years of its execution, his religious views underwent such a change that the man who in the first volume exalts the miracles of "grace" appears a different person from him who throughout the fifth tries in vain to mask his contempt for Christianity in any form. We have not here, in this laborious failure, the real Sainte-Beuve, any more than we have the real Port-Royal. There is, for one thing, an unnatural restraint of his peculiar powers. It has been well said that he seems to have written the book on a wager. Certainly it was concluded either in a spirit of hypocrisy or in that spirit of cynical bravado which is so close a fellow to hypocrisy that it must needs masquerade as its opposite. The tone of the book is neither one of manly partisanship nor one of free, inquisitive, animated exposition. The reader feels that Sainte-Beuve is treading, with steps profane though carefully muffled, through saintly cells and corridors where only moralists and reverent philosophers have the right to feel at home. But his judgments in the sphere of ethics and religion never do carry the same authority as his decisions in matters of literary taste.

After his return from Switzerland, he was appointed, in 1840, librarian of the Bibliothèque mazarine. During this decade of his life, 1834–1844, he was publishing, chiefly in the "Revue de Paris" and the "Revue des Deux Mondes," his "Portraits littéraires" and "Portraits contemporains." In 1845 he was admitted to the French Academy, in the place of Casimir Delavigne, the address of welcome being made by Victor Hugo. He held his office of librarian up to the revolution of 1848. Owing to the troubles of that year, he again left France, accepting a professorship at Liège. His lectures here were on French literature in the early part of the nineteenth century, and resulted in two volumes, entitled "Chateaubriand et son Groupe littéraire sous l'Empire," published in 1860.

Coming back to Paris from Belgium, in 1849, he began writing, for the "Constitutionnel," his "Causeries du Lundi," short informal talks upon literature, which appeared every Monday, as the name implies. To this task he set himself with even more than his accustomed energy and systematic determination. The whole week, except Monday, when he received his friends, was devoted to the labor of research and composition. His secretaries looked up references in the libraries and brought him the needed books and citations. He read thoroughly and repeatedly the author he was to criticise, and dictated his impressions. Upon the arrival of proof-sheets, many additions and changes were made, and it was after he saw his work in print that he gave it those heightening touches which determine the style. This was also Balzac's manner of composition.

Captivated perhaps by Louis Napoleon's insidious *mot:* "L'Empire c'est la paix," Sainte-Beuve allied himself with the Bonapartists, to the scandal of most of his literary associates, and wrote for the official journal, the "Moniteur," after 1852. He also accepted an appointment to a chair of Latin poetry in the Collège de France, but the students, as a demonstration against his political views, refused to listen to his lectures, and he very soon gave up the attempt to read them. They were published in 1857, under the title of an "Étude sur Virgile." His increasing reputation, no less than the Emperor's favor, secured him a position as lecturer at the École normale, but in 1861 he discontinued teaching and applied himself more exclusively to his work for the "Constitutionnel," which offered him a liberal financial inducement. In 1865 he was named a member of the Senate, where, by defending Renan from a charge of atheism, and by speaking in behalf of the liberty of the press, he regained much of the popularity he had lost in 1848. Some of his latest work appeared in the "Temps," a liberal paper much dreaded by the imperialists. By this alliance, and by his conduct in the Senate, he declared himself a member of the opposition. He died after a painful illness, October 13, 1869. Most of his former friends had been alienated from him by his attacks upon them or upon their literary idols, or by his political course, or by his complete renunciation of Christian faith and practice. At his own request his body was buried without religious rites.

There is nothing particularly inspiring in Sainte-Beuve's life if we consider it apart from his work as the author of a minute, comprehensive, and sympathetic history of French literature. His literary criticism alone is his title to fame. If we detach from our conception of him any notion of his being really important or admirable in other respects, our appreciation of his true value will gain rather than lose. His novel and his poetry possess only a personal and relative interest, and his life was open to several grave charges. One of these is that he was a place-hunter and time-server. The imputation cannot be substantiated in this sweeping form. Sainte-Beuve was sincerely conservative, and his early alliance with the radicals was not one to which he was drawn by political affinity at all. He chose his early associates solely because they were men of letters, and in spite of their being republicans or socialists. And moreover, a man may be a monarchist without being either corrupt or blind, although most of Sainte-Beuve's literary friends would hardly have admitted this. Yet there may well have been some moral obliquity in a man of letters who could follow Louis Napoleon in 1852, and for what was considered his servility and short-sightedness in doing so Sainte-Beuve has been severely blamed.

Far more marked were his changes of attitude towards religion; and his final position of cold and passive hostility to Christianity has no dignity in itself and robs of all beauty his earlier postures of calm satisfaction with

Catholicism and then of receptiveness to a rational or Protestant faith. The processes of his development are partly concealed from us, more completely concealed, in fact, than one would expect in a man who wrote so voluminously. But somehow one can hardly believe that his changes of opinion were the result of a foot-by-foot struggle. He probably never went as far towards religious conviction as he professed. His early enthusiasms seem, in part at least, fictitious. This mind of crystal could reflect the studious lamp-light or the vulgar flare of gas-light, and even the light of the sun, but it fixed and held no color.

But these deductions thus made, there remains the great Sainte-Beuve, Sainte-Beuve the literary critic. Here is beauty, consistency, virtue, here is something solid and heroic. His chief critical writings are contained in the five volumes of "Port-Royal," the two volumes of "Chateaubriand et son Groupe," the three volumes of "Premiers Lundis," the five volumes of "Portraits contemporains," the three volumes of "Portraits littéraires," the single volume "Portraits de Femmes," and particularly and best of all in the fifteen volumes of "Causeries du Lundi," and the thirteen of "Nouveaux Lundis." Forty-seven volumes, and yet no mention made of half-a-dozen others which might be classed as literary criticism!

Of the importance of this work I cannot say too much. It is unique among the histories of literature in all languages. It is perhaps the most complete reconstitution of the past ever achieved. With respect of the realities of the seventeenth and eighteenth centuries in France, it is what Balzac deemed that the fiction of the "Comédie humaine" was for the first fifty years of the nineteenth. Sainte-Beuve must be accounted really great as a discoverer, an appreciator, a defender of good literature. There have been critics in whom the passionate love of truth burned whiter and beat more effectually. We think at once of Lessing. There have been others who embraced the round of human action with more comprehensive sympathy and whose *dicta* possess the sanity of perfect intellectual freedom. Goethe is thus universally sound. By leaps of lightning ratiocination Shelley penetrated to the sources of light as no other spirit ever has. Matthew Arnold, who discovered Sainte-Beuve to the English public, had a more earnest spirit, a more general range, and a nobler style than his French contemporary. It is to Sainte-Beuve's honor if he is named at all in such company, when quality alone is considered. But in the matter of quantity and completeness, he has his place as unassailable and unshared as their several places are. His work, too, is more specific, and makes just claims of being wrought out of original and often recondite material. His critical writings, published in daily newspapers and other periodicals throughout a space of forty-two years, disconnected though they are, form, after all, the best history of French literature. Even those who with Zola object to the spirit which informs them, regard them nevertheless as having great "documentary" value. And persons who prefer the synthetic method of Taine, based on philosophical assumptions, must concede the advantages of facility and directness which Sainte-Beuve's untrammelled process affords. When a man begins to read Sainte-Beuve from inclination, relishing him keenly, — when curiosity to learn about the characters of Sainte-Beuve's world is united with appreciation of his critical virtue and his ceaseless and varied charm of speech, the gates fly open which lead into a hundred high-walled gardens of the past, and the initiation into French literature is accomplished.

Yet his work, the best of it, was performed under the conditions of journalism. The book-criticisms we find in old back numbers of reviews and magazines appear generally to our eyes as faded and discolored as the pages upon which they have been lying. Truly the fashion of them has perished. Speaking of his immediate predecessors in French criticism, Feletz, Dussault, Hoffman, all of them writers for the "Journal de l'Empire," Sainte-Beuve says: "We have often heard of the good old times of literary criticism under the Consulate and the Empire. Looking back on that brilliant reign of criticism, we catch ourselves wishing we could see it return again in a form suitable to our epoch. Yet we should be rather surprised if some fine morning we found in our newspapers the same articles on general subjects, the same *feuilletons*, and on the same literary questions, regarded from the point of view whence they used to be so interesting. Notice that I speak here only of those questions and of those subjects which seem eternally in order — Racine, Corneille, Voltaire, La Bruyère,

Lesage. We should be astonished, I say, at the manner in which these subjects were treated; it would seem to us much too easy, much too simple. And in general, when one takes up, after a few intervening years, any old article in criticism or polemics, one is struck with the disproportion between these articles themselves and the effect they have produced, or the memory they have left."

In contrast with these men, and in spite of the fact that like them he did most of his work for daily newspapers, Sainte-Beuve is still a living author. His writings possess qualities which are more common now in history and criticism than they were fifty years ago. They display an erudition and a patience in research which Sainte-Beuve among the first introduced into French literary study and which seem wholly modern. Far from being ephemeral, they are an everlastingly useful repository of information and light.

He began his work in this sort at a time when criticism was more needed than it had been since Voltaire. After the Restoration, from 1815 to 1830, it was felt that an unusual opportunity for national usefulness lay before any writer of genius who could advance a new and attractive theory of life, or better still, breathe a fresh spirit into old forms and clothe the maxims of a venerable faith with the authority of reason. France was intellectually disorganized. Any prophet who raised his voice could gather followers. Society was shattered from top to bottom. The educational views of conflicting parties were irreconcilable. Politically it was felt that the Restoration would only afford time for eruptive forces to gather strength. The Church had lost much power since 1789, and yet its support was supposed to be necessary to the State. Although "the abyss of revolution" was only partly filled, perhaps because this was so, and many institutions were tottering near its brink, the times were more favorable to a conservative than to a radical philosophy of life.

A moderate and rational Catholicism, and a dignified respect for the pre-revolutionary traditions of the country, provided, however, they were combined with an acknowledgment of the unchangeable results of the Revolution,—these were the qualities which it was hoped some great intellectual leader would possess. He might be retrospective, but he must not be retrogressive. We shall not be surprised, therefore, at the welcome given to Chateaubriand and Lamartine. Here were two poets of unquestionable genius. The sources of the great deep seemed to have been opened to supply their inexhaustible speech. They came forward with many professions of power to heal and quiet

> *quella inferma,*
> *Che non può trovar posa in sulle piume*
> *Ma con dar volta suo dolore scherma.*

They had good intentions. They had fervor. They had charm. But alas, they were not great souls, strong in self-command. Ignorant of themselves, and how to rule themselves, they were not able to persuade by example. Lessing, endowed with the very kind of moral greatness which they lacked, was patient and independent even when Germany refused to listen to him, and at last he re-awoke the national spirit in her literature. Wordsworth had this quiet dignity, and stirred England to consciousness of her poetical inheritance. Perhaps if Chateaubriand and Lamartine had met with the same salutary rebuffs which schooled Lessing and Wordsworth at the beginning of their careers, they might have grown to more manly stature of mind. But they were over-estimated from the first. Chateaubriand particularly was spoiled by flattery. He was the pet of women — a drawing-room hero. A false leader was he forsooth in the blundering march France was starting up to make towards faith and peace and wisdom. He had not enough character to stop his ears to the solicitations of the enemy, although accepting the leadership offered him and giving his approval of the plan of campaign. He saw too much to admire in the very foes he had been chosen to attack. He would fain have sworn a truce with them. At one time it was Werther who seduced him; at another "Childe Harold." He could not look straight forward steadily. He is one of the most decent of writers, but one of the most dangerous. In the tell-tale matter of style it is evident enough that a revolution separates him from Voltaire, from Montesquieu, from Diderot — a revolution in taste. He has little of their simplicity, their candor.

One of the clearest proofs of Sainte-Beuve's instinct for discovering literary tendencies is his early perception that Chateaubriand had to be reckoned with as the first great power for good or evil in the thought of the century in France. He readily acknowledged Chateaubriand's wonderful qualities, but, from the first, kept something in reserve. It is interesting to note how this hidden reservation grew in spite of him, through years of quasi-discipleship, until at last it came forth a loud, decided No. The critic in Sainte-Beuve was, even at the beginning of his career, puzzled and excited by a sense of Chateaubriand's weakness.

Sainte-Beuve detected the note of personal vanity and unsoundness in Chateaubriand and the note of intellectual insufficiency in Lamartine. He perceived, dimly at first and notwithstanding his cordial admiration of their power, that even their genius for expression — and it was genius — tempted them into a facile substitution of rhetoric for thought, that, as Lowell says, they were the lackeys of fine phrases. And when he learned to know them in personal intercourse, particularly Chateaubriand, he reached the conclusion that their own sentiments, their own lives, their own greatness, or their own weaknesses and faults, were the sole subject of their poetry, the sole theme of all their eloquence. They published to the world and elevated to the dignity of eternal law the fleeting instincts of their individual natures. In other words, they were sentimentalists. The simplicity of great artists, the unconscious repose of great men, were absent from Chateaubriand and Lamartine. Yet the public was corrupted in turn by those whom it had spoiled. A species of unsound enthusiasm — what the French call *engouement* — followed them. Early in his career Sainte-Beuve comprehended that what his generation needed, in the face of these infatuations, was sane and conservative criticism. He himself was far from worshipping the popular gods. Spite of studied compliment and delicate praise for them, there is nothing in all his writings so evident as his antipathy to Chateaubriand and his distaste for Lamartine. His own enthusiasm was all for the French classics. He appreciated what criticism had done for his seventeenth-century authors. He contrasted the fruitfulness of the writers trained and trimmed by Boileau with the barrenness of many intellects which he saw going to waste about him. "Do you know," he asks, "what has been wanting to the poets of our day, poets originally so full of natural talent, of promises, and happy inspirations? There has been wanting a Boileau and an enlightened monarch, the one establishing and supporting the other. As a result, these men of talent, perceiving that they were in an era of anarchy where discipline there was none, soon began to act accordingly, conducting themselves, not like noble geniuses, or even like men, but literally like schoolboys in vacation. We have seen the result."

To be the enemy of *engouements* and of all charlatanism, Sainte-Beuve pronounces "the true and characteristic mark of a critic." We have seen that it was this dislike of undeserved enthusiasm which first made him suspicious of Chateaubriand. The point is worth noticing, for it was by following the trail his instinct led him to take in this matter that he finally found and wore deep those main paths of literary criticism which he continued with increasing certitude to beat. Chateaubriand was his first big game. In his pursuit of him Sainte-Beuve learned to trust his own impressions, and depend upon his courage, and first practised the critic's arts. His success and the perilous pleasures of the chase had, moreover, the effect of determining, to a large extent, the character of his critical spirit. Sleeping faculties of analysis were awakened in him. Knowing the outcome, it is curious to observe the fascination Chateaubriand exercised over him. It was the fascination of antipathy. In his early essays Sainte-Beuve seems unable to free himself from the consciousness that Chateaubriand will read and criticise him. Although denying him more and more the essential qualities of a true man and a great writer, Sainte-Beuve half unwittingly and all unwillingly acknowledges his supremacy among French authors of the first part of the century. Time has more than justified Sainte-Beuve's reticence and even his boldest attacks, for few literary reputations have suffered a greater collapse than that of this lion of the first Empire, this idol of the Restoration. Lamartine's is another faded glory. So is that of Lamennais. Sainte-Beuve's falling away from these men in the day of their success was at the time often attributed to jealousy or lack of amenity in personal relations. The asperities of his criticism of them were the more noticeable because of the urbanity which is in the main characteristic of his Portraits and Causeries. But we see now that his conservative judgment and good taste were the real causes of his refusal to go with the multitude. In the case of Alfred de Musset, however, for whom he was also severe, time has been more clement.

It was Sainte-Beuve's taste for the best French style, the style of the later years of the reign of Louis XIV., no less than his personal acquaintance with the real Chateaubriand and the real Lamartine, which saved him from *engouement*. His analytical sense was further aroused by his opposition to another of the powerful literary currents of his time, the Gallican, but mystical, Catholic movement of Lamennais and Lacordaire. Although few men have been more liable to enthusiasms, engrossing even if brief, Sainte-Beuve never lost sight of certain definite historical standards. His reconstructive activity was aroused by his love of the best French style, as he found it in Pascal, Racine, Madame de Sévigné, Voltaire, Madame du Deffand, Montesquieu, and by the satisfaction afforded to his æsthetic sense by the tranquil formalism of the *ancien régime*.

The keynote of all his firmest criticism is struck in the following words, which he might with propriety have placed at the head of his collected Causeries: "As for us critics, placed between tradition and innovation, it is our delight to be forever recalling the past with reference to the present, comparing the two and insisting on the excellence of the old work while welcoming the new,—for I am not speaking of those critics who are always ready to sacrifice systematically the one to the other. While the young modern artist swims in the full stream of the present, rejoicing in it, quenching his thirst in it, and dazzled by its sheen, we live in these comparisons, so full of repose, and take our pleasure in the thousand ideas to which they give birth."

This is the whole story of Sainte-Beuve's usefulness. This is his *apologia pro vita sua*. Thus conceived, the office of criticism has the nobility of self-effacement in the cause of public welfare. It is a work of rescue. All about us and within us there are immature and dangerous ideas struggling for acceptance. Weak or pernicious books are appearing in greater number than good ones. Ill-balanced men are pushing forward. If these men, these ideas, these books prevail, and in so far as they prevail, the work of culture is retarded. We know that in the long day Time will sift much that is true from all this false, but that does not make our individual misfortune less if, while we live, the second-best is preferred to the really excellent. Many philosophers would have us believe that man possesses a faculty of such sort as to distinguish intuitively the beautiful in literature, art, and nature. Sainte-Beuve, however, was an experimentalist in this. Most of us are of the same creeping school. We are willing to profit by the opinions of others. We prefer to read the books which have lasted longest and been most in human hands. We are afraid to trust the æsthetic sense. We have our own ideas, to be sure. You may always have thought Byron or the Italian opera unsatisfactory, but it required the weight of a consensus of other people's judgments in the same direction to make you altogether fixed and happy in your decision. For one thing, the critical sense changes with age. At fourteen, we deem "Lalla Rookh" a great English classic. At seventy-five, very likely, we shall have settled down to a steady perusal of Job and Solomon, content with their eloquent inconclusiveness. A healthy criticism, however, bids us take into account the experience of men at all times of life, young men, middle-aged men, old men, and submit ourselves somewhat to their tastes. And the testimony of the dead is at least as valuable as that of the living. It is perhaps the most significant difference between science and literature that the former often deals exclusively with things at present in the world, without a single backward look at historical antecedents, whereas literature not only has its roots in the past, but blooms and ripens there. The study of literature gives as one of its happiest results the sense of the continuity of thought and the dependence of each age upon its predecessors.

> "Can the rush grow up without mire?
> Can the flag grow without water?"

> "Inquire, I pray thee, of the former age,
> And apply thyself to that which their fathers have searched out."

The advice of Bildad the Shuhite is a sound maxim in criticism.

But without literary tradition, without the message travelling down from mouth to mouth, the excellent men of the past become mere names to us. The critic must compel us to read and enjoy. It would occur to relatively few persons, for instance, to read the sermons of Bossuet, were it not for literary tradition. After his death the impression of his power persisted. Even in the eighteenth century his works continued to be read, as of the things which are perpetually in order; and in spite of the changing times his reputation was not sensibly diminished. Finally, through men competent to judge, we learn that he must be placed with Molière and La Fontaine as one of the kings of seventeenth-century literature, and thus persuaded, we cannot help reading him. But do we read him impartially, without prepossession in his favor, coming to him thus at the bidding of others? Most certainly not. Nor is there anything we do judge with godlike freedom. We are entangled in the web of human tradition, ourselves a part of its living tissue. Our skulls are not exhausted receivers, for the accurate performance of experiments, at least not in literary judgment. They are on the contrary almost wholly prepossessed with the ideas of others. If we have companied with good men, both of the living and of the dead, the contents of our minds will be made up of maxims got from sound men and solid books, mixed with a little wisdom and folly of our own. This is a humble view and shocking to theorists.

Like the saying, "Resist the devil and he will flee from you," it may be distasteful to the young, but it finds an affirmative response in every old man's heart. The older a book is, therefore, the more likely it is to have been thoroughly tested, and from this it might be concluded that our reading should be wholly from ancient authors. But various circumstances secure a hearing for the living, in spite of the immense probability against their being worth it. And it is, after all, the old books, the undoubtedly excellent books, which need to be championed. Most people are lazily content to give superiority its due of praise, but what is needed is a critic who shall spur them to the only truly laudatory action possible — that is, to read. Spenser's rank among English poets is high and incontestable. The critic must make people read "The Faerie Queene." How few even well-read people do that! The critic must show that "The Faerie Queene" is at least as important, as interesting, as productive of pleasure, as the ephemeral things upon which we spend ourselves in vain. Mere superiority of knowledge, it is evident, is not the only advantage the critic should possess. He must be an enthusiast. To scrape away at mileposts, found in Yorkshire or on the Rhine, until the time-worn figures appear; to decipher them and show their meaning; to connect these mutilated and abbreviated words with the manifold throbbing life of imperial Rome, hundreds of leagues away and two thousand years ago — this sort of work demands faith and a degree of glorious madness which is akin to genius. Such is the office of the literary critic.

Sainte-Beuve not only saved many seventeenth-century writers from comparative oblivion, but he confirmed the reputation of Bossuet and Saint-Simon, of Fénelon and La Fontaine, of Madame de Sévigné and Pascal. During half a century already, the best French authors have been more read than they would have been without his learned, skilful, and enthusiastic insistence on their interest, their charm, their importance. This is his clearest title to fame. If more humble, possibly, it is a more solid reputation than any he could have won as poet or novelist. His generation was rich in poets and novelists, but would have been poor without him in men of sound taste, capable of appealing effectually to the standards of experience. He enlarged the comprehension of the word "classic," by including in it many works of the sixteenth, seventeenth, and eighteenth centuries, which were practically unknown in 1830, and indicating their excellent features. He made new divisions and discovered hidden relationships. One of his favorite ideas, for example, is that a peculiar quality of urbanity and distinction is to be found in the writings of the generation which flourished in the first quarter of the eighteenth century, so that even the minor letter-writers and memoir-writers of that period, the period of Voltaire's youth, have a singular gift of grace. And while he does ample justice to most of the authors of the earlier and greater era, it is the writers of the Regency in whose resuscitation he most delights. Never before and never after, are there such limpidity of style, such perfect ease, and crystalline perfection, as in Lesage, Vauvenargues, Madame du Deffand, the Abbé Prévost, Fontenelle. Vauvenargues and Madame du Deffand would have been but little known at present, out of France at least, if Sainte-Beuve had not insisted on their worth.

Many persons on reading the Causeries are disappointed to find so little indication of system, or rather of a system. "This is not criticism," they exclaim; "this is history, if you will, but not criticism." They are quite right. It is not criticism as a German professor would understand the term. It is not a philosophy of literature. The Causeries are quiet, familiar, unpretending talks, and rather gossipy, as the word indicates. And the only trace of a method in them is Sainte-Beuve's constant practice of letting each author speak for himself as much as possible. He does not use his authors as mere texts illustrative of some already-formed theory. "I am of those who quote," he says, "and who are not content until they have cut out from their author a good big piece, a fine specimen." He acts on the principle that it ought to be enough to place an intelligent man in the presence of a work of genius; he will appreciate it without much urging. A little modest guidance, some reconstitution of the *milieu*, the explanation of difficulties, and the pointing out of a few details of beauty which might otherwise escape observation — this is usually the proper extent of a critic's duties. It is tiresome to be told just how and why we should be impressed. A doctrinaire never appears so small, nor his system so foolish, as in the presence of a clear, strong, simple man of genius. Such was Sainte-Beuve's theory and such his practice.

He has been much criticised for his habit of making an author's personality and life a basis for judging his works. And at first sight this appears a proceeding of doubtful wisdom. But let us see how he conducts the investigation. He assumes that into a novel or a poem or a drama an author does throw his own personality, and that books are actions. It would be a waste of time, therefore, not to go direct to the heart of an author's life, if we can, rather than shut ourselves up to the consideration of only one phase of his activity. In the end his character will inevitably be disclosed, even through a single work. Why should we not avail ourselves of any short path which leads to his personality, and thus anticipate the sure, but often slow, operation of time? Knowing, for instance, the personal insufficiency of Chateaubriand, Sainte-Beuve felt that it would be exercising too much patience to wait until that insufficiency was also detected by the public in all the sentimentalist's vaunted books. It must be in the books, for it was in the man, and sooner or later a man is revealed, with more or less completeness, in his productions. So he did not scruple to tell what he knew of Chateaubriand as he had seen and heard him. With even less hesitation did he seek to discover the personality of men and women not his contemporaries. It is to this fondness for detailed portraiture that we are indebted for the charming and useful biographies which so many of the Causeries contain. Each author tells his own life, and so far as possible in his own words, which are supported or corrected by extracts from the letters and journals of his acquaintances. Sainte-Beuve's vast knowledge of memoirs, both published and in manuscript, was supplemented by the reading of his secretaries, whom he kept employed in the public libraries of Paris. And much of his feeling for the eighteenth century, a feeling which strikes us as so fresh and immediate, much of his information about the lives of André de Chénier, Bernardin de Saint Pierre, Rousseau, Franklin, Walpole, Gibbon, Mademoiselle de Lespinasse, Madame d'Épinay, and the Encyclopedists, came to him by oral tradition. To mention only one of several lines of communication open to him, he was for some time a frequenter of Madame Récamier's *salon.* She had known in her youth the society of the Consulate, and through it that of the reign of Louis XVI.

Thus we see that Sainte-Beuve's method, which has been often attacked on the ground that it is too much concerned with personality, is in reality the simplest and most natural method in the world. He lets his authors show themselves and speak their own language. He re-animates an ancient *salon*, a group of friends, a family and its connections. He puts us in a position to judge authors as their contemporaries must have judged them, that is, partly from knowledge of their characters and habits. He corrects, of course, this sometimes too narrow view by considering the author's works in a more abstract way, availing himself of distance and the lapse of time, which have their advantages.

But it may be said very truly that all this which I have called his method is only a matter of arrangement. In the writings of other great critics there is a more intimate procedure which may also be termed method, that is to say, the execution of some didactic purpose, the application of some philosophical principle. We seek almost in vain for such a thread of design in Sainte-Beuve's work. It seems as if he were satisfied to bring together other minds, without intruding his own opinions. He has been singularly successful in effacing himself, in not revealing his prejudices, or even his principles. He does not always judge a book or an author. He exhibits; sometimes he interprets too, but not always. He is often satisfied to draw no conclusions after presenting a mass of testimony which he must have labored long to accumulate. To persons in search of decisions made for them by an authority, Sainte-Beuve is baffling and unsatisfactory. But if he were different he would not hold his unique position. His Causeries instead of being chats would be essays. Their buoyancy, their conversational quality, their moderation, their stimulus to curiosity would be gone. Taine's critical bias, which is to make literary and political history illustrate a positivist theory of the universe, attributing the variations of genius and character to material causes, such as climate and soil — Taine's critical bias, which at first seems to tend towards such sound conclusions, leads frequently into error, and has the further disadvantage of making him here and there a tedious writer. Nisard's history of French literature, to mention only one monumental failure, might have been the best work on that subject, if the author had not sacrificed his book and half the French authors to a philosophical theory. He presupposed a typical Frenchman, a typical French style, and a typical French spirit, and estimated all French literature according to its conformity to these ideals. The system is false in its results, for it stamps originality as aberration, and would, in my opinion, exclude, if rigorously applied, such a genius as Rousseau, who had little in common with any conceivable type of a representative Frenchman. It is a system which no man of imagination could have clung to long, though a man of imagination might have invented it. Nisard had an honest, but inflexible, mind. Sainte-Beuve says of him: "He never abandons himself to the current of the artist-natures whom he encounters."

Sainte-Beuve, then, is not hampered with philosophical prepossessions. But this is not altogether an advantage, for one could wish that he were at times more frank in his judgments of literary values, and particularly that he more frequently disclosed his own opinion on points of morality. In short, one feels that he shirks a plain duty and fails to grasp an opportunity. One suspects that the constitutional cowardice imputed to him by his biographers has something to do with this. Towards the close of his life his indifference to moral distinctions is fairly cynical, and is doubtless due in part to practical defiance of a moral obligation in his own conduct. How he could help being more pronounced, it is hard to see. To most of us it is unsatisfactory to read much in any field, passing in review a long list of men and women, of actions and ideas, without co-ordinating and speculating. We do need some philosophical thread. We are not long content with the mere accumulation of facts; we must draw conclusions. And one feels disappointed sometimes that a man so well furnished with facts is so seldom disposed to aid in the fulfilment of this natural desire. Sainte-Beuve admits his reluctance. "I am a man of doubts and repentances," he exclaims. In the generous Causerie in which he welcomes a fellow-critic, Edmond Scherer, then knocking for admittance to the Parisian world, Sainte-Beuve says of him, as if accepting the contrast: "He does not feel his way; he does not hesitate. He is a firm, solidly-based intelligence, which has in itself a standard whereby to measure exactly every other intelligence. He is a peer, rendering verdicts upon his peers. He is a veritable judge."

In matters of taste and style Sainte-Beuve has himself the trenchant confidence of decision which he remarks in his young rival. But Scherer's boldness was in another sort of judgment. He had just published his "Mélanges de Critique religieuse," which included essays on authors whom Sainte-Beuve would have considered in his province too, such as Joseph de Maistre and Taine, but whom he would scarcely have cared or dared to discuss from a definite position in philosophy and religion, as Scherer did. Sainte-Beuve doubted the ability of the French public to appreciate the serious treatment habitual to Scherer, and, with a sort of *gran rifiuto* which is painful reading, betrayed his own distaste for any criticism which attempts to go beneath the surface of life. It is characteristic of timid people to under-estimate the courage of others. Sainte-Beuve's tone in this Causerie is just a little that of a *boulevardier revenu de tous les préjugés*. One grows weary, in the end, of the French habit of shunning serious conversation. A man may be devoid of theory and yet be capable of rendering very valuable judgments. One would be grateful to Sainte-Beuve for more of them. The unfortunate aspect of his abstention from deciding points which he, better than any other man, was qualified to settle, is apparent when he passes over, without condemnation, the ruinous corruptions of the age of Louis XIV. For example, he gives us a portrait of Mademoiselle de la Vallière which, if uncorrected by other reading, might make us believe that she was in all respects a pure, high-minded woman, and one of the loveliest ornaments of an innocent and noble era. Not that I think every historian of literature is called upon to extract a moral from the lives of his authors. But Sainte-Beuve's position was peculiar and his duty obvious. He was making the men and women of letters from 1661 to 1715 live over again for the benefit of a generation which, as he declared, needed standards of life. By touching lightly upon evils whose existence and whose tainted and contaminating results he well knew, he failed to represent seventeenth-century life as it really was, in France, and the standard loses its authority. He should have had the courage to publish boldly his opinion of the enormous corruption of a reign whose greatness has been over-estimated, not without harm to the French character. Like most other French critics and historians, he caressed so daintily these false ideas that if we had not Saint-Simon to tell us the truth, we might miss the whole point of the timely and necessary revolt which began with the eighteenth century.

Alluding to the subjects of his lectures in the École normale, from 1857 to 1861, Sainte-Beuve makes a distinction which he has happily not always observed, between his work as a teacher and his work as a critic. The two offices are quite distinct, he says, "the critic's being, above all things, the search for what is new and the discovery of talent; the teacher's, the maintenance of tradition, and the conservation of taste." Yet it is worthy of remark that most of the subjects of his Causeries and Portraits were chosen without reference to works which had been recently published. Less than half the Causeries du Lundi are book-reviews. In his practice as critic he was performing more than ever the duty which he lays down as that of a teacher; he was maintaining tradition and conserving taste.

His selections appear at first sight singular. In the fifteen volumes of the "Causeries du Lundi," there is not one essay on Molière or Corneille or Racine; but, there are two on Bussy-Rabutin, three on Madame de Maintenon, two on Dangeau, two on the Marquis d'Argenson, and two on Madame du Deffand, while the company of courtiers and worldlings is further increased by single Causeries on the nieces of Mazarin, Saint Evremond and Ninon de l'Enclos, Mademoiselle de la Vallière, Hamilton, author of the "Mémoires de Grammont," Madame de Caylus, Chaulieu, La Fare, the Duchess of Maine, and Madame de Pompadour. The persons whom Sainte-Beuve most delights to introduce are those who not only have written, but have made some stir in the world by their swords or their tongues or their bright eyes. The more serious side of court life is, however, not neglected. Indeed Sainte-Beuve has seldom gone deeper into detail than regarding Bossuet, to whom he dedicates three of the Causeries du Lundi, and Fénelon, whom he discusses in two. On the whole, if you look through the entire series of Lundis and Nouveaux Lundis, you will be struck with the large proportion of persons who were more celebrated for other things than for literary achievement. This is one of the most attractive and valuable features of the Causeries; they furnish the environment of the great French authors. We are admitted into the best circles of intellectual French society, in which Boileau and Racine, Fénelon and La Fontaine once moved, and by which the character of their work was conditioned. It is remarkable also how largely the cultivation of letters under Louis XIV. was confined to the aristocracy. Of course the exceptions will occur to every one. But numerically the advantage is on the side of the nobility. Moreover, when a *bourgeois*, like Regnard, made himself distinguished, he was quickly admitted into court circles.

I dare not fail to quote here two paragraphs from Sainte-Beuve, which are models of simple, compact French, and models also of a sort of feminine grace in avoiding a difficulty. They stand at the head of the Causerie for Monday, July 8, 1850, on Madame du Châtelet. Nothing could be more delicately expressed. He makes one feel that it is scarcely fair to blame him for a defect to which he is not blind himself, and about which he can reason so delightfully.

"I must say a few words of explanation in reply to more than one question put to me in various ways. What is my purpose in returning with such pleasure, in my Causeries, to these seventeenth and eighteenth century subjects? Is it my aim to propose them as models? Not precisely; but I wish, above all things, to aid in maintaining the line of tradition, without which nothing is possible in good literature; and so what is simpler than to try to fasten tradition to the last link of the chain? Even if many things were already corrupted at the end of the seventeenth century and throughout the eighteenth, the language at least was still good; prose especially was yet excellent when it was Voltaire or his near neighbors who spoke or wrote. I wish therefore that we could be carried, that I myself, first of all, could be carried, back to the reign of that clear, simple, fluent language. I would that in commerce with these witty men and women of a century ago we might learn to converse as they used to converse — with sprightliness, with politeness, if that be possible, and without too much emphasis. One of the defects of newly-constituted societies (which have their good qualities, to be sure) is to wish to date from themselves alone, is to be disdainful of the past, is to be fond of system, and consequently rude and inflexible, or even a trifle fierce. I should like to see our younger generation cultivate and modulate themselves, and acquire, little by little, this simpler style, these lively and facile expressions, which used to be reputed the only truly French form. As for the morality of the eighteenth century, there are many cases in which I censure it. If there are some readers (and I think I know some) who would prefer to see me censure it oftener and more roundly, I beg them to observe that I succeed much better by provoking them to condemn it themselves than by taking the lead and seeming to try to impose a judgment of my own every time. In the long run, if a critic does this he always wearies and offends his readers. They like to think themselves more severe than the critic. I leave them that pleasure. For me, it is enough if I recount and depict things faithfully, so that every one may profit from the intellectual substance and the good language, and be in a position to judge for himself the other, wholly moral, parts. These, however, I am careful not to conceal."

It is evident from all the quotations I have

made, as it is patent on every page of his works, that Sainte-Beuve was a classicist, a conservative, that he felt the dignity and beauty of the past and acknowledged its authority. He was keenly alive to fine shades of difference. He had the aristocratic instinct, and preferred the best to the second best, the noble to the common, the interests of a select few to the interests of the mass. There are well-bred books, just as there are men of born distinction. The republic of letters is not a very happy phrase if it is supposed to imply the equality of books. What we see is, rather, an aristocracy ruling triumphant over middle class and lower class alike. It is a hereditary system, too, and the descent of books, at least of those which belong to the most powerful families, can be traced for many generations. Does any one suppose that the fables of La Fontaine are without ancestry? They may not show their family quarterings, but in the literary herald's office their lineage is duly recorded. Of the prolific race which came down from remote ages through the Decameron, who can number the offspring? That lively blood betrays itself in Chaucer and tells again in Shakespeare. In the world of books it is no disgrace to be a tuft-hunter.

Stronger than the most selfish parasite's fondness for a duke, is Sainte-Beuve's instinct for a grand or an elegant style. He has wonderful facility, also, in detecting whatever is unnatural or false. His favorite device for disabusing his readers of exaggerated respect for any book was to quote some violent or sentimental passage from it, some strained metaphor, some weak or pretentious phrase, and then ask if Voltaire could have used such language, or if the simple diction and polished thought of Madame de Sévigné were not preferable. He employed this process very effectually against Chateaubriand. But sometimes it was not adequate, and he occasionally did injustice to a man of peculiar genius, as we have seen in the case of Musset. And he entirely failed to appreciate Balzac. It could hardly be expected that such a lover of classical perfection, such a lover of form, should approve of Balzac's style, which is often overstrained. The critic was repelled also, as delicate souls will always be, by the want of real gentility in Balzac's thought. There is much of it that is imposing, but nothing that is distinguished. As in his life, so in his creations, and pre-eminently in that most intimate of all a man's creations, his style, there is something monstrous, uncouth, something which betrays a lack of refinement. Social intercourse of the right sort will sometimes produce sufficient polish, even where the man is low-born or naturally rude, and Balzac was neither. But he did not enjoy early enough the advantages of companionship and friendship. Sainte-Beuve could not but be shocked by Balzac's curious combination of insufficiencies and excesses. He did injustice to the sincerity of his character. And the naturalist school will never forget that Sainte-Beuve, thus rendered blind to Balzac's power, also failed to see in him the great novelist, the greatest novelist of France. For all his eccentricities, Balzac was, of course, no charlatan. He did his share of posing, but he was, of course, no mountebank. It is a pity he could not have had Sainte-Beuve for a friend and taken his advice in matters of form, at least. But it is also to be regretted that Sainte-Beuve underestimated the tide-like sweep of that great talent.

From the persons and books he disliked, it is apparent that Sainte-Beuve's especial antipathy was for declamation, the sounding brass and tinkling cymbals of discourse, the oratorical habit, the love of mere rhetoric, the want of simplicity, excess of emphasis, or to sum up all in his own word, *la phrase*. This he considered the worst element of bad style, and a sure indication of vulgar taste.

As a true disciple of the prose writers of that chosen period of his, the end of the seventeenth and the beginning of the eighteenth century, Sainte-Beuve is annoyed by vagueness, and his own works are marvellously clear. He is more concrete than is usual with critics. He has the precision of a fencer, with all a fencer's grace. He has the French faculty for fine insinuation. His Causeries read like skilful conversations; they abound in delicate approaches and feigned withdrawals. His good-humor and self-command are well-nigh perfect. His flashes of indignation are so rare as to be always welcome. But he is for the most part imperturbable, serene. Not many men, having to write a piece of literary criticism once a week for half a life-time, would have developed so few crotchets and refrained so entirely from arbitrary or tyrannical judgments.

Despite his vast and minute information, there is in Sainte-Beuve no mere pedantry of letters, no boasting of mere research. He does not throw up barriers of erudition between the reader and the author who is under discussion, but tries, rather, to remove every obstruction. He does not think it beneath his dignity to sketch broad, popular outlines of the lives and works of his subjects. He is never content with furnishing a mass of recondite facts. In each of his sketches you can refresh your knowledge of the author who is being criticised. It is not, as a rule, taken for granted that even the main features of his life will be known to you. Sainte-Beuve treats these elementary matters with a patient enthusiasm, an originality, a charm of language, which make them always fresh and delightful. Thus one of the first effects he produces is to acquaint the reader personally with a man or a woman.

He somewhere uses the words *savant* and *érudit* in such a way as to show the beautiful distinction between them. A man may be *érudit* and stuffed with learning, yet it may be all congested in his brain, and he but a crude scholar. A *savant*, on the other hand, has better possession of his faculties and knows how to open his treasures to the world. Knowledge will not swamp a man, unless he be deficient in active energy — or power of expression, which is almost the same thing. Sainte-Beuve was distinctly *savant*. He is neither a scientist nor a philologist in his treatment of literature; he is a man of letters. His solicitude is that he may interest us in the literary aspect of French history — the influence of personal character upon books, and the effect of books upon the national life. It remains for a more philosophical mind to interest us equally in the historical aspect of French literature.

It is natural to expect of a critic so intimately acquainted with these details that he should, at least towards the end of his career, draw valuable conclusions as to the distinguishing qualities of the French race, and the relative value of its intellectual product. Sainte-Beuve answers but insufficiently this expectation. We find among his works a small number of essays on foreign authors. They show that he possessed breadth of sympathy and capacity for accommodation. But they are relatively few, and moreover they nearly all treat of writers who had a large share of the French spirit, and lived much in France, or wrote in French. Such are Lord Chesterfield, Benjamin Franklin, Gibbon, and Frederick the Great. No history of French literature would be complete if it failed to take account of these. Sainte-Beuve is still, therefore, in his original circle when he speaks of them. To be sure, he has essays on Goethe, Dante, Firdousi, Theocritus, Virgil, and Pliny the Elder, but yet it must be said that he does not abound in those rich comparisons between different literatures which constitute much of the value of Arnold's critical writings and Schlegel's. In this he is a true Frenchman, for his countrymen are none too hospitable to foreign ideas and none too well acquainted with other literatures than their own. They are, after all, much more insular than their neighbors across the Channel. When Sainte-Beuve does, however, venture upon comparisons, he shows an admirable catholicity of spirit, and we can only regret that he so seldom let his mind go forth on foreign travel. From the rare excursions he allowed it to make, it returned with booty characteristic of the lands it had traversed. Thoroughly French though he was, and limited by some French prejudices, his essay on Cowper, for example, proves that he could appreciate an English type of intelligence absolutely foreign to his countrymen — incomprehensible to many of them. In reading this Causerie one feels that perhaps Sainte-Beuve's practice of abstaining from international comparison does not indicate lack of knowledge or appreciation on his part, so much as on the part of the public for which he wrote. It is chiefly when thinking of this restraint and of what we lose by it, that one regrets the peculiar circumstances of his authorship.

For after all, and it is not a reproach, we must conclude that Sainte-Beuve was a journalist, and that although his success was made possible by his close contact with the public, it was also limited thereby. Fortunately the roots of his development were struck in academic rather than bohemian soil. He won his great and unique celebrity by happily combining in himself the professor, the journalist, and the man of the world. Other men in his situation commonly suffer an abasement of their talent and a levelling of their style. In him the more solid elements of the mind strengthened with years, and there is little of an ephemeral character in his work. From the very limitations of his position he gained advantage, for to whom would he be so useful if his flights were longer or his range more general? He is so close to his hearers and in such an easy attitude that it would be ridiculous for him to sermonize or prate. So he simply talks — in the first person singular, as if seated with a group of listeners around a table full of books. He speaks with an easy and well-bred familiarity, with vividness and endless variety. It is a lively, instructive, polite conversation, on the many forms of his subject, for he had but one, and that is French literature. To study this, to purify, propagate, and defend this is his great concern.

What shall be, then, our final word about the utility of Sainte-Beuve's criticisms? In the first place, and whatever else may not be said, he furnished an easy approach to almost every French author of the seventeenth and eighteenth centuries, and reconstructed, with much charm and truth, many literary and social groups, from the Hôtel de Rambouillet to the *salon* of Madame Récamier. He checked the *engouement* of his contemporaries for Chateaubriand and Lamartine, who were being elevated to a position of authority which was not theirs by right. He in the main judged soberly of Hugo and Béranger, and steadied, if he did not stop, their oscillations before an altogether too complacent public. He was more severe with Musset than even Time himself has been. His sense of proportion and love of restraint blinded him to the heroism of Balzac's titanic struggles, while he justly cried out against the unsound literary taste and the often grotesque style of the great novelist, who made upon his sensibilities much the same impression a lifter of weights at a fair produces upon the nerves of a delicate woman. In opposing his criticisms to Balzac's popularity, Sainte-Beuve was attempting to check the ocean-tide, and this is his only notable failure to appreciate genius. What he was unable to do with respect to Balzac, he accomplished very sympathetically in the case of George Sand. He was one of the first to celebrate the irresistible charm of her warm and generous speech, strong and sweet as the sunlight. But after all, if it is only to award praise or blame among contemporaries that critics write, they may often do well to spare their pains, as the examples of Balzac and Musset show. Useful as it frequently is, such work is not of incontestable value. An incomparably greater office of criticism is to establish the reputation of the few supreme writers, no matter of what age or in what tongue, to smooth the way up to them, and allure men into their august and benign presence.

BALZAC

BALZAC

THE acts of a human being are memorable in so far as they benefit mankind. Some of these are acts of conscious devotion, and they are the noblest. Others are performed for the pleasure of doing things well. In all cases, usefulness to the world is the standard by which the world judges. Works of art are no exception. Indeed, works of art are simply the most notable examples of disinterested effort to be useful. Art for the world's sake is the only art the world cherishes. The self-pleasing fancies of the dilettante are short-lived. The esoteric distinctions of cliques and schools make us say of a book or a picture that it is provincial or pedantic or affected. What unfailingly marks the highest products of great artists is the quality of being permanently serviceable. Very little poetry that still passes for such was written with any other inspiration. But it is a question whether equal disinterestedness has presided over the writing of more than a small number of novels.

Immediate personal profit, in the shape of reputation or money, has not often been attainable by writing poetry, and poets have generally looked rather towards fame, which is the reward for priceless and imperishable service only. On the other hand, fortunes have been made by novelists, and against the eighteen pounds paid for "Paradise Lost" and the salt-savored bread which Dante ate, we have the $80,000 earned by Victor Hugo with "Les Misérables," and the $120,000 earned by Benjamin Disraeli with "Endymion" and "Lothair."

Balzac is the greatest French novelist. One-third or one-half of the best French novels are his; and from him dates nearly all that is excellent in the theory and practice of his successors. Since his day the men who have done most for the art of fiction in France, the men who have developed it and kept it vital, have been his disciples. He expressly formulated, and on many a page he illustrated, an unimpeachable doctrine of realism. Fidelity to the truth as derived by actual observation, or capable of being tested by observation — this, Balzac taught, is an indispensable quality in a novelist. He is the greatest French novelist, but wrote some of the most inartistic books in all French literature. He was the father of the realists; yet, for many of his works his sons are tempted to disown him. Moreover, he conceived and carried out, to an astonishing extent, the idea of representing in fiction the life of his time in France, so that no essential feature should be lacking; and he did all this in such wise that the picture, though complete in almost every feature — complete beyond praise and beyond parallel in literature or any other art — is a distortion of the truth!

There are two keys to this enigma. One is a certain imperfection in the man. The other is a certain peculiarity of the times in which he lived. In the man two incompatible natures struggled for mastery. He was one of those composite characters in whom the conflict of opposite tendencies does not produce a resultant of forces, but each operates alternately. By virtue of his better nature, he was a great genius, original, courageous, industrious, disinterested, and possessed also of those secondary charms and graces which often accompany the noblest gifts. When this nature prevailed, there was no meanness in the man, and especially no weakness; he was generous, buoyant, clear-sighted, a thorough artist, felicitous in thought and word. But when the noble part of him was in abeyance, when desire for quick recognition and great wealth was uppermost, Balzac presented but the vulgar type of a man living selfishly.

When the artist-nature, weary with the day's work, or despairing of perfection, laid down the pen to recuperate, this coarser spirit would often take it up and write abominably, to make money. The money-maker, being the less scrupulous writer, was less easily tired, and filled many pages in these stolen intervals; his hand was heavy, his wit coarse; he had no taste. Hard, unenlightened, rationalistic, declamatory, a Parisian shop-keeper *endimanché*, the commercial Balzac was responsible for the want of distinction which has been so often remarked in the great master. And for whatever want of fidelity to truth has been remarked in him, for this also the commercial Balzac was in large measure responsible. What did the commercial nature care for theory? What does "business" ever care for theory? In theory Balzac was a realist, and most of his greatness comes from his being, in the main, nobly faithful to his theory. Where he departs from the truth as capable of being tested by observation, he occasionally startles us with a strange exhibition of spiritual insight, but more frequently falls miserably below his own level of interest and style. Laying aside the figure of a dual-nature in Balzac, we may say that he was a man who saw the truth and wrote the truth like a sublime artist, except when he yielded to a temptation to which he was peculiarly liable, and set the love of money before the love of serving the world, or the love of doing great things well.

Leaving out of account the anecdotes, probably in large part legendary, which his biographers have seen fit to record in place of much-desired fact, and making what use we can of his sister's brief and charmingly indulgent sketch, and of his published letters, and his various portraits, we may gather some idea of Balzac as he was in early manhood, and again twenty years later. The former is the critical point with him. Here, for the last time, we may perceive his original disposition, and with this in mind we may estimate the influence over him which external things came to exert.

In 1819 the young Balzac, aged twenty, and enjoying for the first time the pleasures of independence, wrote home from his attic in Paris, in this gay strain: "Ah, sister, what torments does the love of glory not inflict! Hurrah, then, for the grocers, for they sell goods all day, count their gains at night, finding relaxation from time to time in a dreadful melodrama — and are happy. Yes, but they spend their lives amid cheese and soap. So let us rather cry, Hurrah for men of letters! Well, but they are poor of purse and rich only in pride. So come, then, leave both alone, and Hurrah for everybody!"

And again the same brave whistling a few weeks later: "I have bad news to tell you about my housekeeping; my work is a foe to cleanliness. This rascal Myself" (a cheerful figment of his imagination, who attended to all the menial service) "is getting more and more negligent. He does n't go downstairs to buy provisions more than once in three or four days, and then patronizes the nearest and worst-stocked shops; the others are too far off and the fellow saves his steps; so your brother (destined to be so celebrated!) is already nourished exactly like a great man; that is to say, he is starving." And a little later: "I feel to-day that wealth does not bring happiness, and that the time I am spending here will be for me a source of pleasant memories. Living as I please, working to suit my own taste and in my own way, doing nothing if I wish, dreaming on into the future, which I paint in rosy colors, thinking of you folks at home and knowing you happy, having Rousseau's Julie for my mistress, La Fontaine and Molière for friends, Racine for master, and the cemetery of Père-Lachaise for my walking-ground — Oh, if this could only last forever!"

The boy whose spirits overflowed in these refreshing outbursts had been taught to appreciate freedom by a childhood of unusual repression. He was born in Tours, May 16, 1799, and christened Honoré. He died at Paris, in 1850. His parents were in easy circumstances, and had him brought up by a peasant nurse in the country till he was four years old, and at seven sent him away again, to a boarding-school at Vendôme. Here he passed seven years without a vacation, and, being a great reader and not a diligent scholar, and withal very unhappy, was accounted a dull boy. His health breaking down, which is not surprising, he was taken out of school, and lived at home in Tours until the family, in 1814, removed to Paris. Here he attended private schools for about two years, and later heard lectures at the Sorbonne and the Collège de France. In his eighteenth, nineteenth, and twentieth years he read law and spent a twelvemonth each in the offices of a solicitor and a notary. His father saw a good opening for him in the legal profession and insisted on his practising, but the young man rebelled. M. Balzac the elder, as one may gather, was a selfish, obstinate old man, with an *idée fixe*, that of preserving his health and living as long as possible. Honoré persisted in his refusal, and at last wrung from his father permission to live alone in the city and try for a certain time the experiment of a literary occupation. He was provided with a small allowance, and ordered to assume a false name and avoid being recognized. Meanwhile the family had removed to a suburban town.

When Honoré wrote the exuberant letters quoted above, he had therefore only one care in the world — to write something which should justify his course and secure his independence. His tone is natural, high-spirited, courageous. His ideal is pure, his heart uncorrupted. "My only grief," he exclaims, "is the small amount of talent I discover in myself. . . . All the toil in the world cannot produce a spark of genius. . . . And mediocrity be hanged!" The product of several months of ecstatic labor was a drama, "Cromwell," which failed to satisfy the family tribunal, and young Balzac spent most of the next seven or eight years under the parental roof and authority. But he won meanwhile a limited toleration by writing stories which were paid for. He looked back, however, with bitterness, to a lonely childhood and a repressed youth, and in 1828 he said: "From the harsh restraint in which I have lived I have acquired at least a wild sort of energy and a horror of the yoke, of which you can form no idea." The stories by writing which he partly emancipated himself were published under various pseudonyms up to 1829. There were forty volumes of them! He perfectly well realized that they were valueless except in two respects: they brought him a little money and they enabled him to learn how not to write.

In 1822, in the midst of this trying apprenticeship, he so far lost confidence in his genius, or was so led astray by belief in his business capacity, that he began to speculate, and presently found himself the unfortunate possessor of a printing-office, a type-foundry, a publishing-house, all bought on credit, and a quantity of unsalable books, popular editions he had made of Molière and La Fontaine. From this time on, the commercial Balzac, to resume our figure, was an indispensable companion of Balzac the artist, and took advantage of the situation to thrust himself ever forward. The necessity of paying off debts gave undue importance to the trading instinct, which may have existed before in Balzac, but which till now had not been prominent. The scorn with which the trading-classes in France have always been regarded by the classes who are supposed to be above them, is not so difficult to understand as a similar feeling in America would be. The lower French *bourgeoisie*, with many exceptions, of course, are hard, methodical, avaricious, inhospitable to ideas. They do not travel, they do not read, their interests do not extend beyond gain and physical comfort, and their sympathies are limited to their own families.

All the bigotry of business is theirs. An unenlightened patriotism completes rather than modifies the selfishness of the men, and the women, for almost their sole impersonal interest, have recourse to a tread-mill round of formal religious observance. It has been said, with much apparent truth, that French men of letters and painters and sculptors speak disdainfully of the *bourgeoisie* because it is from the *bourgeoisie* they themselves have escaped. Unhappily the artist in Balzac never escaped the uncongenial yoke-fellow. Judging from his letters, the commercial aspects of novel-writing filled his mind almost to the exclusion of every other interest, except when he was actually engaged in composition. He knew no leisure. The harshness of his character, the crudity of his thought, are consequences of a raging activity which allowed no time for reflection. The man and his work lack relief, harmony, ripeness. He had no time for retrospection, for friendship, for enjoying literature. His life, from the turning-point in or about 1822, was one continual debauch of labor. Grinding toil subdued his manhood. A large part of his work is the production of a weary mind and lacks spontaneity.

One characteristic citation from Balzac's later correspondence will suffice to show what a change came over him in twenty years, and how he was then struggling. In a letter to his sister, dated 1839, he writes: "I hope this week to have completed the famous payment, and even to have enough money to settle the most pressing smaller claims, leaving only about ten thousand francs unpaid. All is going well, and I shall have something to tell you Friday or Saturday. The Renaissance Theatre capitulates and offers me fifteen thousand francs in advance. I have finally brought them to these terms. . . . Last week I wrote fifty-five printed folios. I must do as much this week. I have slept only forty-five hours in ten days, but not without risk." There is little else in his letters of this period than such discourse as this, only it is often more feverish and sometimes acrimonious. And the ten thousand francs that stand between him and freedom have a way of suddenly increasing. With every smile of fortune he blossomed forth in fresh extravagances, bought more furniture, committed more follies, borrowed more money, engaged himself more deeply with publishers. One who has recourse to Balzac's letters in the hope of learning the secrets of the novelist's art, or of breathing an atmosphere of noble thought, will be disappointed, but may acquire much information about notes of hand, compound interest, discounting, renewals of bills, contracts, and litigation.

But what! we might say; shall we blame a man for trying, by every power with which he is endowed, to pay his debts? Is it not esteemed honorable in Scott that he spent himself to be free from pecuniary obligation? There are two kinds of difference, however, between Scott's attitude and Balzac's, in this matter, and at any rate, it is not so much the right or wrong we are considering as the cause of certain imperfections in Balzac's works. In the first place, Balzac differs from Scott in that he relished the excitement of business. We cannot altogether believe what he says on this subject. He protests again and again that business is killing him, while apparently it is half his life, and half his pleasure. He was a speculator by instinct, and no sooner got his head above water than he plunged in again. Another difference is that Balzac's flashy tastes and luxurious habits were often responsible for his financial embarrassment. He was notorious for his extravagance, and for the barbaric splendor of his living. In these things Scott was a gentleman, and Balzac neither better nor worse than a French business man of the class whom French gentlemen despise or affect to despise.

The time and place in which Balzac came to maturity have also much to do with his defects. From his sixteenth year he lived in an atmosphere of speculation, when large fortunes were being made, owing to the rise in French government bonds, and the general revival of business, coincident with the Restoration. In spite of the monarchical character of the restored government, many results of the Revolution were not seriously impaired, and the era was in reality democratic, or rather plutocratic. Thousands of families from the lower orders of society, having had the prudence to invest their money in national funds between 1814 and 1820, realized enormous profits, and so came into sudden prominence during the next decade, when securities were high. It was an era of peace, the first peace of considerable length that France had known for a generation. It was also an era of invention and discovery all over the world, an era of great industrial development; and the shrewd, frugal peasantry and *bourgeoisie* were able to employ their savings to advantage, for the rate of interest was high. Moreover, to a man of business instincts, to a novelist singularly curious about money dealings, it was, of all times, the best for observing the careers of dishonest people. There had been frightful peculation during the recent wars. The confiscation of Church property and of the estates of *émigrés*, the contract system of supplying vast armies, and finally the abuses of royal favor in behalf of the restored nobility, had left a deep and mixed deposit of fraud on every side. It was not unreasonable to suspect a dishonest origin for almost every fortune, great or small, in France. An observer might be excused for becoming cynical. A richer field for the social geologist never existed. Not only in this matter of wealth, but in regard to social elevation, marriage, titles of nobility, public offices, legitimacy of birth, sincerity of moral, religious, and political professions — all, in fine, that goes to make up the inner tissue and the outward show of security and success — men felt they were walking on hollow ground.

It is evident that to a mind like Balzac's, in which the noble interest of an artist was inextricably complicated with vulgar curiosity and personal greed, this mixture of the social strata must have proved inviting. He was attracted by the singular problems which the times presented, and also, unfortunately, by the opportunity he saw for enriching himself. Before him, although Voltaire had made large sums by his writings, and Beaumarchais had made money his chief concern, it is doubtful if any great French man of letters had seriously set about to gain a fortune by literature. The Encyclopedists were content to live, if necessary, in extreme privation, rather than turn their eyes from what seemed to them a sacred task. And the great writers of an earlier day, as well as many of Balzac's contemporaries, were of the noble caste or imbued with its traditions, which discountenanced trade. Of nobility, in the sense of rank, Balzac had none, notwithstanding the particle *de* which he had the presumption to assume.

Balzac was the man to accept the challenge of these circumstances and cope with these temptations. In bodily presence he might at first pass for insignificant. He was only five feet tall and was decidedly fat. His countenance lacked grace, benevolence, and dignity. But power resided there, extraordinary, indubitable power. The broad, knotted forehead, the heavy eyebrows converging violently downward over the root of the nose, the flaming brown eyes, the pouting lips which rose at the corners, the small, well-moulded chin, spoke him a determined, self-confident man, and capable of profound concentration. It is a face from which humility is entirely absent, but one would hesitate to pronounce it irreverent. Curiosity sits at the window in his vivacious eyes. Toil has bruised and swollen the space about them and drawn creases downward from his nostrils to his chin. Cheerful energy, not so much godlike as diabolical, smiles out from the lips. On those who knew him, his character made an impression in keeping with his face. They thought him strong, but not fine; jovial, but not witty; terribly in earnest, but not noble. They tell us, with more or less innuendo or apology, that he was sensual, gross, vain, fatuous, and obstreperous; that his tastes were crude; that money was his idol. But they tell us too, and the world knows it without their testimony, that he cherished a high theory of the novelist's art; that before all things else he loved reality; that he worked unremittingly, as no other man of letters ever worked, harder than ordinary human flesh and soul can endure or should be expected to endure.

This powerful but defectively organized being set for himself an extraordinary task, from which a more refined nature might have shrunk with apprehension of its difficulty or a keener sense of human weakness. It was no less than to reproduce, in a series of novels and stories, the totality of contemporary French life. Human society, he said, contained several thousand types. Just as the different species that constitute the animal world may be represented by typical specimens, so these human types sum up in themselves the varieties of mankind. "French society," he declared, "was to be the historian; I was to be only the secretary. In drawing up an inventory of the vices and virtues of society, collecting the principal facts about its passions, painting its characters, choosing its chief events, and composing types by uniting the features of several homogeneous characters, perhaps I could succeed in writing the history which has been neglected by so many historians, the history of manners and morals. With much patience and courage I should produce for nineteenth-century France that book which we all wish we possessed, and which Rome, Athens, Tyre, Memphis, Persia, India have unfortunately not bequeathed to us in regard to their civilizations." He continues in the same confused style, embodying a kind of mysticism in terms drawn from the vocabulary of natural science, and with not a touch of humor or real humility, to say that the crown of his work shall be its philosophy. He will explain the universe. "By adhering to this strict reproduction, a writer might become a more or less faithful, more or less successful, patient, or courageous painter of the human types, might narrate dramas of the inner life, might be the archæologist of social furniture, the nomenclator of the professions, the registrar of good and evil; but if I would merit the praise to which every artist should aspire must I not study the reasons, or the reason, of these social effects, catch the meaning hidden in this immense concourse of figures, passions, and events? Finally, after having sought, I will not say found, this reason, this social motive force, should I not be bound to meditate on the principles of nature and see in what respect societies conform to, or depart from, the eternal rule, the true, the beautiful?"

Here was a programme which only a Frenchman could have formed. It is too complex, too systematic, too audacious, to have sprung from any other people. In its odd jargon of science, the Prospectus of the "Human Comedy," of which these words are the gist, is thoroughly characteristic of the second quarter of the nineteenth century. What is Balzacian about it is that the promise was fulfilled! At least it was fulfilled far more completely than any other man could have fulfilled it, and abundantly enough indeed so far as quantity goes. And in such an undertaking, of course, quantity is as important, almost, as quality. The Prospectus was written in 1842, and referred not only to works then as yet unwritten, but to the best of what Balzac had previously published, since 1828. The ninety-two novels and shorter stories, and the five dramas, which constitute the vast work to which it stands as preface, are the "Human Comedy." Only about one-half or two-fifths of Balzac's published writings come under this head. Yet the "Human Comedy" comprises no less than ten thousand closely printed pages, in which more than two thousand persons figure. All these characters have life. All have individuality. Many of them are intricate and subtle, being counted among the most complicated men and women in fiction. And a large number appear in two or more of the books, without, in any instance, losing consistency. The story-telling, or fabulation, is almost equally rich, though of less remarkable quality, as compared with what other novelists have done. But in a third respect — with regard to the amount of intellectual food incidentally supplied in the shape of descriptions, reflections, and the like — the "Human Comedy" is wonderfully abundant. Even Scott and Tolstoi are thinly provided in comparison. The question may arise whether the individual narratives do not suffer rather than gain by this wealth of substance. Certainly, however, it is important as a contribution towards the object of the "Human Comedy," which was to make and explain an imaginary cross-section of French life in Balzac's day.

Broadly considered, then, the "Human Comedy" comes marvellously near being what Balzac aimed to make it. It is the most astounding feat in literary history. The title suggests comparison with the "Divine Comedy" of Dante, and notwithstanding that the one is divine and the other flatly and unmistakably human, notwithstanding that the one is pure art and the other is art mixed with plain day-labor, there is some equality between the two in the mass and variety of life represented. Of course we must not expect to find the heady promise of the Prospectus fulfilled absolutely. There is a limit even to titanic powers, and we shall see that it is doubtful if, in the highest sense, it was fulfilled at all. For what though the details are abundant and in the main correct, if the total impression be spoiled by over-emphasis of the beautiful or the ugly, the good or the bad? And in this matter of emphasis, of a just balance between effects, of a broad experience of life truthfully expressed, the question of an artist's personality is everything.

Let us not begin at the wrong end, and say that, because Balzac is known to have been a coarse, money-loving man, therefore his view of French life is false. What we know of his character is after all not very much. But it is reasonable to accept this little as an explanation, in part, of the generally acknowledged inadequacy of his work, in its total aspect. The specific defects have been noted by almost every reader who has published his observations. In fine, it is agreed that the moral color of the picture is too dark. Or, to test Balzac by his own standard, he has chosen a larger proportion of evil types than life really warrants. The temptation is usually of the contrary sort, and Balzac is said to have been particularly severe, in his conversation, towards writers who had, as he expressed it, *l'hypocrisie du beau.* He certainly did not err in that direction himself. Merely in numerical excess, let alone his manifest partiality for them, his rascals and charlatans, his complex intriguers, his vicious and selfish women, have an unnatural advantage over the honest people. And this is not all, for it frequently happens that when he tries hardest to make a hero he makes a dandy, or a cad for a gentleman, or a person of very soiled and dubious virtue for a lady. His balance is unfair, for he was a pessimist; his tone is low, for he was unacquainted with the high levels of life, with real gentility, with simple, uncompromising morality, with heart-felt religion. We are reduced to the paradoxical conclusion that the "Human Comedy," while a feat of almost superhuman difficulty and marvellously performed, is a failure as a picture of reality, although its strength lies in its realism. Critics of Balzac's own day were, with the exception of George Sand, not as much overcome by his power or convinced of his sagacity as most readers of our time are. Perhaps this is because we have seen so much genius, so much devoted talent, in his successors, produce results that have never equalled the results he produced. Undoubtedly, too, we are less capable than the men of 1850 of appreciating the difference between life as it actually was in the first half of the century and life as Balzac depicted it.

Happily, it is not necessary to read the whole of the "Human Comedy" in order to enjoy Balzac, though only by reading all of that huge work can we fully appreciate his enormous power and awful industry. Few of its component parts lose anything by being read separately. Many of them are superbly well executed; at least an equal number are among the dreariest, or the unloveliest, or the most profoundly immoral books in the French language. Taine, in his remarkable essay on Balzac, acknowledges that a great part of the "Human Comedy" is not such reading as a man of culture, accustomed to good society, and scrupulous as to whom he admits to intimacy, would relish. But he makes the claim in Balzac's behalf that the reading habit has spread downward into the uncultivated and undiscriminating levels of society, and that Balzac is none too vulgar for the modern world. Conversation that would make the *habitués* of an eighteenth-century *salon* raise their eyebrows may be welcome enough, Taine says, in a men's club of the nineteenth century. This is a singular defence of Balzac's defects, for literature is not quite the same thing as social converse. We look to literature, even the least delicately nurtured of us, for something more interesting, nay, for something more elevated, than common events and common talk. Precisely here is the value of books, that they enable us to choose more refined or more remarkable or more lively company than life generally offers to any one of us. In his best books, Balzac has amply proved that novels which do this can nevertheless be written in strict conformity to every essential rule of realism. Moreover, those of his books that are likeliest to please a club-room of commercial travellers, or other specimens of *l'homme sensuel moyen*, violate outrageously the realistic principle of verisimilitude.

The mob of fashionable libertines, police spies, sentimentally debauched duchesses and countesses, rich and marvellously beautiful actresses and courtesans, of shady bankers, picturesque usurers, bohemian actors, idle and diabolically clever journalists — all this gaudy riff-raff which whirls perpetually before us in the "Human Comedy," spoiling half its novels, all these so-called Parisian types of the *demi-monde* and "high life" — Rastignac, Maxime de Trailles, Lousteau, la Palférine, Lucien de Rubempré, Ronquerolles, de Marsay, du Tillet, Félix de Vandenesse, Léon de Lora, des Lupeaulx, Nucingen, Magus, Gobseck, Nathan, Vautrin, Corentin, Peyrade, Florine,

Florentine, Coralie, la duchesse de Maufrigneuse, la vicomtesse de Beauséant — these and a score of others like them are as improbable as they are depressing, not to say degrading. To contemplate their vices cannot refresh the spirits and improve the character even of Taine's imaginary clubman. But, indeed, they seem mere caricatures of reality, and we are forced to suppose that even the great Balzac had his head turned by the glamour which, in the eyes of nearly all Frenchmen, emanates from people who are actually the silliest part of the population. Some of his novels must be accounted entire failures, because in them these figures, whom he dotes on, predominate. "Le Lys dans la Vallée," of which he had a high opinion, is the most falsely sentimental book in the world, the most glaring example of what manners and morals an ill-mannered and immoral author considers noble and elegant. "Splendeurs et Misères des Courtisanes" is a phantasmagoria of impossible infamies, a stupid melodrama played under the dreary glare of lime-light. These two long novels, the three tales known collectively as "L'Histoire des Treize," and several shorter pieces, among them "La Femme Abandonnée," "Une Fille d'Eve," and "Les Secrets de la Princesse de Cadignan," are so false in almost every particular, and, moreover, so needlessly disagreeable, that the world of art would lose nothing by their annihilation. "Béatrix," opening with a masterly piece of description, which is not too long for those who love perfection of detail, and with an interior scene worthy of an old Dutch painter, falls off presently into Balzac's worst manner, in endless, dull pages of sophistical meddling with questions of adultery.

Other books — for instance, "Le Contrat de Mariage" — are merely slow and painful. Another, "Ursule Mirouët," a favorite with some readers, is, perhaps, the best example of how Balzac's personal deficiencies have betrayed him. It is a study, evidently intended to be gently modulated and charming, of a young girl brought up in maidenly innocence by a wise, dignified old physician, her uncle, in whom Balzac plainly tries to create a type of a gentleman. The attempt in both cases is clumsy. Balzac is never so hopelessly at sea, never puffs and splashes so wildly, as when, in this novel, and also in "Modeste Mignon," he strives to produce these two indispensable types. The man knew no reserve himself, and how should he paint modesty and dignity? His books are a mountain of evidence against the French system of bringing up and marrying girls, their hothouse education being represented as weakening their moral tone and leaving them an easy prey for designing men; yet when he would depict a girl less trammelled than her sisters by what he plainly considers the absurd conventions of French society, he makes her pay for the gain by a loss of charm. In not a few of his other and less defective works there are passages untrue or meretricious, where Balzac, the man of affairs, secured temporary possession of the pen, and either showed his own bad taste or wrote to please people of bad taste, in order to make money. Such excellent books as "La Rabouilleuse" and "Le Père Goriot" and "Le Colonel Chabert" are not easily spoiled, but they have grave defects, every one of which a man of taste, who did not entertain exaggerated ideas about money, would have avoided. Money, with ignoble ways of earning, hoarding, and spending money, is the very substance of Balzac's books, as it seems to have been of his personal life. And there is nothing so inimical to gentility, nothing so foreign to art, as a constant preoccupation with profit and loss.

What remains that is solid and perfect in Balzac? Much remains. And he appears more wonderful when we consider how great the best part of him is, after so many deductions have been made. In the first place, he has described more things and done it, on the whole, more excellently, than any other French novelist. It is often without grace or lightness of touch, to be sure; he spares us no details; he inventories and classifies even the unessential; and for some readers his introductory chapters are a sort of purgatory or quarantine. But the true Balzacian relishes these passages. They are done with such perfect mastery! They bear witness to so much observation, by a mind endowed with rare intellectual curiosity, to which no human interest was foreign! They are unsurpassed examples of the power possessed by keen senses, a strong imagination, and an exact appreciation of words, to evoke not mere fleeting phenomena, but intricate and substantial masses of reality. Balzac does not catch at life's fluttering skirts as she hastens on, but arrests her bravely, holds her fast, and looks her narrowly in the face. Not only do these great descriptive passages give us knowledge, surer than what guide-books impart, more minute than our own untrained eyes and ears would furnish, of French towns, and streets, houses, rooms, furniture, clothes, figures, faces, speech, and gestures, but they draw from us cries of pure æsthetic satisfaction, they are so perfectly performed. A fugue of Bach, a rondo of Haydn, are not more beautiful in workmanship. And the same virtuosity which gives us the opening chapters of "Eugénie Grandet," "Le Père Goriot," "Le Curé de Tours," "La Recherche de l'Absolu," "Béatrix," and "La Femme de Trente Ans," ennobles a thousand minor passages with bars of exquisite precision.

Then, the consistency of his characters! We may not believe that he proportions goodness and wickedness, beauty and ugliness, as they exist in nature; we may think he takes delight in evil and allows it to predominate; we may observe that he blunders and seems unfamiliar and ill at ease with the persons whom he would fain make generous and simple-hearted and well-bred. But in spite of all this, his characters are true to themselves; they hang together, they breathe and move and live. There are some exceptions, which have been mentioned, but we have two thousand cases in proof! This is where genius plays its part. This is where Balzac again stands foremost among French novelists.

Apart from the conventional types already noted, his characters are almost all not only firmly conceived, but lifelike. The unusual distinctness of his minor persons, particularly servants, has often been remarked. He has made few attempts to describe children; but his old people are as individual and as really old as Rembrandt's wrinkled money-changers. Youth, maturity, age, both sexes, and all ranks, professions, trades, employments, and all temperaments, all shades of guilt and innocence, of ignorance and wisdom, are portrayed as if Balzac had himself possessed a dozen lives. But where wonder seizes us is when he concentrates his terrible analytic gaze upon some intricate, strange, or passionate soul joined to a body inscribed fourfold, like a palimpsest, with a long life's indelible effects. Baron Hulot, Père Grandet, Balthazar Claës, Philippe Bridau, were no easy knots to untie. And Balzac not only made them, but took them apart again. A less laborious, but a perfect and very delightful figure, is the Chevalier de Valois, in "La Vieille Fille." In a small number of his works Balzac attempts a task perhaps the most difficult of all — to analyze abnormal or diseased natures and still keep touch with earthly reality while attributing their peculiarities not only to natural, but to supernatural causes. It is a question whether the adventure was not unfortunate. Balzac himself was satisfied, and many excellent judges relish, for example, "La Peau de Chagrin."

In the third place, and it is a point scarcely less essential than his achievement in description and in character creation, there is much discourse in Balzac that might have found place in essays or dissertations on history, civil government, social economy, agriculture, education, religion, and other high topics, but which, being more than all else a novelist, he embodied in his stories. It has been said frequently that these excursions injure the fictions in which they occur. But the true Balzacian, again, delights in them and finds them profitable. An astonishing wealth of information is here cast at our feet, the very thing which, in the Prospectus, Balzac said he aspired to do. Superficial readers may be repelled, and indeed Balzac is never easy reading, but there is much matter in him which is of great value now and will be priceless for the future historian of French life.

They might be described as philosophical passages were it not for the ill use Balzac makes of the word philosophy. He fell an easy victim to every pseudo-science and every pretentious system of thought emerging half-formed from speculative minds, and veiling insufficiency with jargon. All the great mystifications which at that time were so rife in Europe found in him a curious, if not a self-surrendering, disciple — phrenology, telepathy, mesmerism, Swedenborgianism. Had the Mormons been able to catch his ear, be sure they would have struck his fancy. If by philosophy we mean large speculation about the common affairs of men, or a gift of analysis, Balzac was no insignificant philosopher. But of philosophy in any more definite and scholastic sense, he had but a slight tincture, for all his vast claims. It is hard to think he was a deliberate impostor in this matter; he was only an unconscious charlatan. But the result of his high opinion of his own metaphysical genius is that for hard-headed people "Louis Lambert" and "Séraphita" are impossible reading, and "La Peau de Chagrin" little short of impossible. "La Peau de Chagrin," moreover, suffers from the faults that ruin "Splendeurs et Misères." The psychological interest of "La Recherche de l'Absolu" is of a high order. The mind of Balthazar Claës is in a pathological, perhaps an unnatural, condition, and his pertinacity in delusion wearies us, but we may be thankful that the allegory does not protrude excessively, as it does in "La Peau de Chagrin." Symbolism, which is so effective in a very short story, as in "Jésus-Christ en Flandre," one of the noblest short stories in the world, is unendurable in a long work. It is worth observing that good fables are always brief.

There is philosophy, however, of the practical sort, an attempt to express and co-ordinate general views of life, in many of Balzac's novels, and notably in "Le

Médecin de Campagne," "Le Curé de Village," and "Les Paysans." The chief of these opinions — and it will be observed that they support each other and form a system — are in advocacy of constitutional monarchy, a nobility kept from decay by laws of primogeniture, development of French commerce by government, and finally Roman Catholicism recognized as the state religion. At the present day this may seem a very much discredited or at least reactionary programme, but somehow Balzac contrived to give it a wonderful appearance of vitality. The first half of "Les Paysans" is an extreme example of how far a novel may not be a novel at all, and yet be interesting. Indeed, it is safe to say that whoever enjoys the deeply speculative first part will be comparatively indifferent to the second part, in which the story proper at last begins to stir.

But the novels considered thus far are all imperfect works. The perfect works have been reserved for the last word. Whoever wishes to read something of Balzac and cares little about toiling through the long valley of the shadow which the whole "Human Comedy," despite its cheerful name, really is, whoever wishes to enjoy Balzac, will do well to begin where we shall end, with the indubitable, the illustrious successes of the great master. They are numerous enough. No other French writer, perhaps no two or three of them together, can offer so long a list of splendid novels: "Eugénie Grandet," "César Birotteau," "Le Curé de Tours," "Le Père Goriot," "La Femme de Trente Ans," "Un Début dans la Vie," "La Rabouilleuse," "Le Colonel Chabert," "L'Envers de l'Histoire contemporaine;" and of short stories: "Jésus-Christ en Flandre," "Un Episode sous la Terreur," "Le Chef-d'œuvre inconnu," "La Messe de l'Athée," "L'Auberge rouge," "Le Réquisitionnaire," "El Verdugo," "Un Drame au Bord de la Mer." This list might easily be lengthened, but to shorten it were an ungracious task. It contains more vigorous intellectual substance than all the rest of French fiction put together. In these pages live two or three score men and women endowed with distinct individuality and at the same time standing as types of the race. Things visible are represented here so that we seem to see them. The human mind and conscience are here analyzed as if they were visible things. Here we have few lapses of the artist into a mere seeker of selfish interests. Here are few traces of venality either of purpose or temperament. A high earnestness here prevails, and we feel that the truth is being told about life. A sense of awe overcomes us, as in the presence of an irresistible power, for through all these books quivers the mighty will of their creator, in painful effort, in exalted earnestness, compelling where it cannot charm.